GunDigest
SHOOTER'S GUIDE to the
AR-15

RICHARD A. MANN

Published by

Gun Digest® Books, an imprint of F+W Media, Inc.
Krause Publications • 700 East State Street • Iola, WI 54990-0001
715-445-2214 • 888-457-2873
www.krausebooks.com

To order books or other products call toll-free 1-800-258-0929
or visit us online at www.gundigeststore.com

ISBN-13: 978-1-4402-3847-5
ISBN-10: 1-4402-3847-2

Edited by Jennifer L.S. Pearsall
Designed by Jana Tappa
Cover Design by Nicole McMartin

Printed in USA

For Guthrie

I first met James Guthrie during a visit to the headquarters of the National Rifle Association. I was there to talk with the editor of *Shooting Illustrated*, which is the NRA's newsstand magazine. Guthrie was at his desk wearing Carharts, a button-up shirt, and what I've now learned was very likely the only tie he owned. Best described as a country boy from Georgia, Guthrie and this hillbilly hit it off.

Shortly after that, Guthrie left the NRA for a career as a freelance gun writer. Some questioned his logic, but I understood that D.C.'s Beltway was no place for a guy like Guthrie. He did well, and it wasn't long until he was covered up with work that included guest-starring on a television show called *Modern Rifle Adventures*, which aired on the Sportsman Channel and was a show all about the AR.

While Guthrie was always a blast to have around a campfire or on the range, and while some of his writing have helped to educate thousands hunters and shooters, I believe his greatest contribution to the shooting sports and, now, his legacy, will be how he aptly demonstrated that the AR-15 was a viable sporting rifle that even a good old country boy could put to good use. During the many episodes of *Modern Rifle Adventures* that aired, shooters and hunters got a look at one of the most unforgettable personalities I've ever met; I'm sure that was contrary to what many viewers assumed, but Guthrie wasn't acting. What you saw was both real and what those of us who knew him expected every time we were around him.

Just about six months before Guthrie passed away, he attended a bachelor party/'gator hunt for a mutual friend. My son, Bat, who was 12 at the time, met Guthrie, and they immediately connected. Bat was drawn to Guthrie, because he was a man living his dream and having fun and because Guthrie could go from adult to teenager in the same sentence. Guthrie liked Bat, I think, because he saw some of his own gregarious personality in him. Guthrie told Bat he laughed like a little girl, Bat told Guthrie he could outshoot him and, after dinner one evening, they were found in the parking lot talking about girls and seeing who could jump the highest. That was the magic inside James Guthrie. He infected everyone with his smile and energy.

All writers hope they can leave a legacy with their work, and Guthrie undoubtedly touched many with his words in print and in film. What I'll remember most are the smiles and laughter he etched on so many hearts. I'll forever think of Guthrie any time I laugh beside a campfire or hunt with an AR, and my life and the lives of many others, including my son's, are richer for knowing him.

Although this book pales in comparison to the positive introduction to the AR rifle Guthrie gave so many viewers on *Modern Rifle Adventures*, where he continually upstaged his older and balding deadpan host, it is has come to me that this is my opportunity to try to fill the void Guthrie left. As it is, it's just a drop in the bucket we will all be trying to fill for a long time; if James Guthrie were still here, he's the one who should have written it. Then, you could have learned all Guthrie knew about the AR and experienced his one of a kind, Southern-influenced, country boy humor at the same time.

I was hunting in Africa with friends, when I learned Guthrie had died. Hurting, we all did what Guthrie would have done, had he been in our shoes: we went hunting and we shot stuff. It could have only been better if we'd been hunting with ARs, and with him.

I miss him.

Give me an "A!" Give me an "R!" What's that spell? AR! What's that stand for? ArmaLite! Well, that's what it stood for until Richard Mann had his say.

I'll bet that ArmaLite's Eugene Stoner never imagined how powerful a statement those two simple letters, side by side, have made over the last 60 years. Mr. Stoner completed the design of his revolutionary AR-10 select-fire rifle, chambered in 7.62x51mm NATO, back in 1955. A short while later, Stoner's chief assistants at ArmaLite scaled down the original design to create what the world knows today as the 5.56mm NATO-chambered AR-15.

That bit of trivia aside, since you have picked up Richard A. Mann's *Shooter's Guide to the AR-15*, you either recently purchased your first AR, you're on the hunt for the first of many AR-platform rifles or, perhaps, you're looking to improve your overall knowledge and ability to effectively run such rifles. Doesn't matter, you're in good hands with Richard, rest assured! As a gun magazine editor for Harris Publications, I've had the great pleasure of working with Richard for more than a decade. He is a tried and true, been-there-done-that contributor guys like me reach for, when we're in a jam for strong editorial content.

Richard sort of coined the phrase "America's rifle," when referring to the AR, and that's something you'll come to completely understand every time you reach for the *Gun Digest Shooter's Guide to the AR-15*. And reach for it you will, every time you need help learning how to operate, maintain, and service your AR, and even when you just want to better understand how one works. You'll also reach for *Shooter's Guide to the AR-15* when you're prepping for your next hunt or shooting competition, to learn how to select the best optic or cartridge for your AR. Richard's a master, when it comes to cartridges, ballistics, and handloading, so, if that's part of your future game plan, again, Richard's book will get you started down the road in the right direction.

I like to say, "Your AR is not your AR until you dress it for your personal shooting endeavors." Translation: You'll reach for *Shooter's Guide to the AR-15* when it comes time to add AR furniture and accessories like super-slick handguards and grips, AR-dedicated optics and backup sights, specialty buttstocks, and a ton more! Richard has tested them all through the years, and his integrity in this business is unwavering. Trust me, he'll steer you in the right, commonsense, and practical/tactical direction that will save you hard-earned money in the long run.

When it comes to feeding your AR, it's best to remember the old saying "Waste not, want not." With ever-rising ammunition costs, overall demand being at an all-time high, and suppliers having difficulty keeping up, no savvy rifleman wants to blow through their ammo while trying to zero their rifle. Before you next range session, you'll want to reach for *Shooter's Guide to the AR-15*, so you won't waste your lead downrange. Ammo-saving efforts will come by way of reading up on how Richard sets you dead straight on things like zeroing the AR, proper shooting positions, sound training and practice drills, and a host of other weapon-craft secrets.

What you've just read merely scratches the surface of what this new book brings to the AR shooter's bench—and that's just for *new* shooters. Before long, you'll be reaching for *Shooter's Guide to AR-15* and flipping to the chapter where the author shows you how to build your very own AR rifle from scratch!

With all that reaching for this book that you'll be doing, might I make a suggestion to you before you lock and load? Stash a copy of *Gun Digest Shooter's Guide to the AR-15* in your range bag or AR rifle case. Heck, you might even want to buy a second copy to keep handy by your in-home gunsmithing station. It's bound to be a helping hand when you most need one.

Anyway, welcome to the exciting, sky's-the-limit world of AR ownership. Be safe and enjoy reaching for all the AR stars that Richard has dished out for you in this great title.

— *Nino Bosaz, Editor In Chief* AR Rifleman *and* Rifle Firepower *magazines*

ACKNOWLEDGMENTS

Napoleon believed that, with enough ribbon, he could have taken over the world. His observation that "A soldier will fight long and hard for a bit of colored ribbon" is true still to this day. While the production of a book such as this does not compare to fighting a war or to taking over the world, it is an undertaking that could not be completed without soldiers, and I would like to thank the following for their service to this project: Jorge Amselle, Nino Bosaz, Kyle Brown, Mike Capps, Cody Carroll, Chris Ellis, Jack Ellis, Adam Heggenstaller, Jessica Kallam, Bat Mann, Drema Mann, Amy Miller, Buz Mills, Pat Mundy, Travis Noteboom, Linda Powell, Dave Starin, Karen Starin, Eddie Stevenson, Bryce Towsley, John Vehr, Len Waldron, Bill Wilson, Caylen Wojcik, and Larry Weeks.

I would also like to thank the soldiers of the United States military for their service. Without them, this book could not have been written, because there would have been nothing to write about. It is those soldiers who have trusted and relied on the AR, and who will continue to do so, I owe my gratitude to more than anyone else. Their sacrifices are what allow us to remain free.

ABOUT THE AUTHOR

Richard Mann was born in West Virginia, and grew up with a rifle in his hands. During his professional career as soldier, police officer, and special agent, he worked as a small arms instructor and has trained thousands of military and law enforcement personnel, as well as many civilians, in the proper application of small arms.

Richard is currently a contributor to all the major firearms periodicals published by the National Rifle Association, as well as many other firearms and hunting magazines. He has written several firearm related books and operates a blog, www.emptycases.com.

Richard Mann

Though he hunts, shoots, and travels all over the world, he still lives on his private shooting range, Shadowland, which is located in deep in the hills of West Virginia. Like Richard, his wife and son are both graduates of Gunsite Academy, and his two young daughters love to shoot, too. If you stop by to visit, expect to be met at the gate by a huge German shepherd with ADD and a very protective Rhodesian ridgeback.

ABOUT CONTRIBUTOR JORGE AMSELLE

Jorge Amselle

Jorge Amselle reviews and tests many ARs each year and is intimately familiar with the companies that make them, their backgrounds, and what they do best. Amselle is a contributing editor for Harris Publications (*Combat Handguns, Guns and Weapons for Law Enforcement,* and *Special Weapons for Military and Police*) and NRA magazines (*American Rifleman, Shooting Illustrated,* and *InSights*). He has more than 20 years experience in communications and as a press spokesperson as a public policy expert on education and civil rights. His articles have appeared in *The New York Times, The Wall Street Journal, National Review*, and other national publications.

CONTENTS

SECTION 1: THE AR

SECTION 2: THE AR INSIDE AND OUT

SECTION 3: AR SIGHTS AND ACCESSORIES

SECTION 4: WEAPON CRAFT

SECTION 5: EXTRAS

CHAPTER 1

AMERICA'S RIFLE

AR does not stand for "Armalite rifle" or "assault rifle" anymore. The AR is "America's rifle."

For more than 100 years, America's most iconic rifle has been the lever-action. No other rifle begs to be picked up, have the action worked, or tweaks that little bit of cowboy in us all. But, to steal a phrase from Bob Dylan, "The times they are a changing." The AR is quickly becoming the long arm of choice for American gun owners.

For those who believe the spirit of a rifle can only be held deep within the marriage of oil-finished walnut and blued steel, this can be a hard pill to swallow. I'm no different. There has not been and never will be a rifle that can touch my soul and warm my hands like Grandpa's old .30-30. It's no different for me with trucks. His old '69 Chevy pickup … now *that* was a real truck. I've owned several, but that bench seat, three on the column shifter, and two-gauge dashboard has been forever etched in my memory. Still, I would not trade the heated seats, XM Radio, power windows, four doors, and the high ground clearance of my modern pickup truck.

Machines—rifles or trucks—evolve faster than humans. With some things, we readily accept change. Few would give up their iPhone for rotary dialers, party lines, and pay phones. I doubt you know anyone who longs to trade their 55-inch, high-definition flat screen for a black-and-white floor model.

Advancements in luxury and convenience we warm to quickly; things challenging passions we experienced when we were first learning to hunt or shoot have a harder row to hoe. An AR is no different than a smartphone. It can do many things. Its versatility is unmatched. By simply changing upper receivers, you can go from a coyote-calling rifle in .204 Ruger to a 300-plus-yard big-game rifle in .30 Rem. AR, or you can slap on a .22 Long Rifle upper and have anything from a squirrel rifle to something ready for a day of fun at the range with the family.

The ability to do most of the jobs an American rifleman would ask of it isn't the only reason for the rise of the AR. Our country has been at war for 10 years. Just as it was after World War I, when servicemen came home convinced that Colt's 1911 was a handgun they could believe in, just as it was after World War II, when they came back convinced that the .30-06 and the M1 Garand had saved the world, today's veterans come home knowing they can trust an AR. Our military's

adoption of and our veterans' experiences with the Colt .45 made it the most trusted handgun and pistol cartridge in America, and their experience with the M1 Garand is the reason semi-automatic hunting rifles became trusted, as well. With the AR, it's no different.

Let me go on record and say that I've never picked up an AR and felt something stir deep in my soul. It has never helped recall a childhood memory, and holding one has never left the scent of wood smoke, boot grease, and a hunter's breakfast in my nose. When I pick up an AR, I feel something different. I feel I have a very capable tool in my hands. I feel I'm holding a precision-engineered instrument capable of allowing me to shoot to my utmost potential. But most of all, I feel like a free American.

Holding and shooting an AR helps me connect with the idea that—at least for now—in this country I can own a rifle,

Just like the 1911 convinced American veterans it was the greatest fighting pistol of all time, so has the AR brought another group of veterans to a new level of understanding.

and owning a rifle is what differentiates a citizen from a subject. No, there's no walnut or blued steel, and I know a cowboy never carried anything like this. But I also know a cowboy never owned a repeating rifle he could use to do what I can do with an AR.

The beauty of the AR (America's rifle) is that buying one, owning one, shooting one, or hunting with one doesn't mean you have to give up on all your others. I still own more lever and bolt rifles than ARs. I continue to hunt with both, especially when

The AR-15 may not, at this moment, evoke memories of the past like a lever-action rifle does. However, 30 years from now, it will do just that with those shooters becoming acquainted with it today.

*The AR has become America's most popular firearm,
mostly due to its versatility, but also partly due to politics.*

I want to connect to something special in my past. There will always be a .30-30 or a lever gun of some sort in my closet—just as there will always be an AR in there keeping it company. The AR represents the evolution of the rifle and this country. Let freedom ring!

To both many non-gun people and gun owners alike, the AR represents something different, even sinister. Certainly, there have been a few incidents where criminals perpetuated heinous acts while using an AR. As bad as this is and as isolated as these incidents are, what's worse is that there are some who believe these guns were machine guns. This is partly because they look like military weapons, but mostly because those folks are uneducated when it comes to firearms and simply don't understand the difference between a semi-automatic rifle and a fully automatic rifle.

This lack of understanding reaches further than you might imagine. My neighbor is a hunter and has been most his life. He also owns numerous firearms that he uses for hunting and for recreational shooting. When the Federal Government was last attempting to pass a ban on ARs or similar firearms, he was visiting me and the topic came up. He commented, "I think they need to pass that ban. Nobody should have a machine gun."

I was flabbergasted and, at first, didn't know what to say. After all, I thought my neighbor was a "gun person." I thought about it for a moment, then said, "The assault weapons ban they are attempting to pass has nothing to do with machine guns. It is about semi-automatic rifles, specifically those that *look* like military rifles. They want to ban rifles that operate the same way as your Ruger 10-22 or your Browning deer rifle."

My neighbor looked at me all wide-eyed and said, "Really? That's not what I thought it was all about."

And there you have it. It's not so much that a portion of the American population is *against* the AR as it is they do not *understand* what the AR is.

To understand the place the AR holds in America, it's important to understand history. In the early days of the Vietnam War, the U.S. military was trying out its new service rifle, the M14. This rifle might be best described as a more compact, magazine-fed version of the M1 Garand. By today's battle rifle standards, it was heavy at more than 10 pounds when loaded. It was also long, at almost four feet.

Even while this new rifle was being fielded, a man by the name of Eugene Stoner, who was working for Armalite, was developing another rifle that was designated the AR-10. It fired the same .308 Winchester (7.62 NATO) cartridge as the M14. Another version of this rifle, designated the AR-15, was also being developed, and it fired a .22-caliber cartridge. Both designs were submitted to the U.S. military for consideration, but were ultimately rejected.

In 1959, Colt's purchased the rights to both the AR-10 and AR-15 rifles from Armalite. Colt's was successful in getting the U.S. military to take another look at the AR-15 and, in 1964, it was ultimately adopted. It offered several advantages over the M14. It was lighter by about three pounds and it

was also about six inches shorter. Add to that the fact the AR-15, which the military had designated the M16, fired a more compact cartridge, and it made this new service weapon better suited to jungle warfare. Soldiers could carry a smaller, lighter rifle and more ammunition for the same weight burden of its predecessor.

Colt's began offering a civilian version of the M16, which it called the AR-15. The main difference in these rifles was that the M16 was capable of fully automatic fire, while the AR-15 could be fired only in semi-automatic mode.

The AR-15 was a bit slow to attract civilian shooters. This was mostly because it was specifically set up for use with open sights; it was difficult to mount a scope to the rifle.

Without ease in scope mounting, sport shooters and hunters had little use for the rifle. It wouldn't be until the 1990s that the AR-15 platform would become uniquely modular and the flat-top receiver was born.

Eliminating the carry handle on the AR-15 and replacing it with a section of Picatinny rail made scope mounting easier. The development soon led to free-floating handguards that were also decorated with sections of rail. The military's approach was the M4 carbine, which is really nothing more than an M16 with a shorter barrel, flat-top receiver, and railed handguard.

With the advent of the flat-top receiver on the AR, civilian shooters finally started to see the advantages this modular weapon system offered. It could be set up for a variety of

The AR-15 was the civilian, semi-automatic version of the fully automatic M16 used by the military.

The U.S. military has transitioned away from the longer barreled M16 to the more compact carbine version of this platform, which is designated the M4. (DefenseImagry.MIL photo.)

shooting endeavors and was extremely versatile. To support this interest, a vast cottage industry of aftermarket AR accessories developed. Some were in response to military and tactical needs, but others were driven by sport shooting and hunting applications.

In response to a school shooting in California, where the perpetrator used a military-styled semi-automatic rifle—and with support from the anti-gun crowd—Congress passed the 1994 Assault Weapons Ban. This law banned the sale and manufacturer of semi-automatic rifles that had certain cosmetic features, features indigenous to the AR-15. One of these features was a magazine that could hold more than 10 rounds. This was about the time the term "AR" was contrived to mean "assault rifle," when all along it has stood for and continues to reflect the company that originally designed it: Armalite.

The ban would last 10 years and, statistically, history has proven it had no impact on violent crime. Nor did it do anything to curb the sale of or interest in AR-type rifles. The ban expired under the watch of President George Bush, in 2004. When Barak Obama was elected president, civilians, expecting a reinstatement of the ban, began to purchase AR-15s and similar firearms in record numbers. No such new legislation was offered until after the 2012 election, when a freak of a human committed a mass murder at an elementary school in Connecticut.

The tragedy at Sandy Hook was immediately followed by a massive push by the anti-gun crowd and the President to institute another so called assault weapons ban. It ultimately failed in Congress, but a variety of states passed their own ban of sorts—and still others were passing laws supporting the ownership of the very firearms the proposed ban would make illegal.

More and more shooters, both men and women, are learning about the modularity and versatility of the AR platform.

In essence, all this political jockeying served to do was reinforce the AR as the most popular firearm in the United States. Shelves were empty of ARs, ammunition, and many other types of firearms for months. And, as more and more Americans bought ARs in various configurations, more companies building ARs and AR accessories emerged.

Yes, to some extent, the AR has become the most popular firearm in the free world due to politics. But, as shooters purchased ARs, maybe only because they thought that next week or next month they may not be able to, more shooters learned about the versatility the platform offered. Now, the demand for ARs is higher than it ever has been for any other firearm at any time (and the demand for AR ammunition and AR accessories is just as high). Americans are learning that, with the AR, they have one rifle they can use to do about anything they want to do with a rifle. Companies have been trying to design and sell products like this since the free marketplace was established, but nothing short of a claw hammer has come as close to providing everything a section of the consumers might want as has the AR. All this history is what makes the AR no longer the Armalite Rifle or an assault rifle. It is indeed what makes the AR America's rifle.

CHAPTER 2

THE WORLD'S MOST VERSATILE RIFLE

Entering the millennium, it was clear that the gun of the future would be the AR.

I believe that, as a civilian consumer and like most American shooters, I wasn't drawn to the AR until the flat-top version became available. Sure, as a combat rifle, the standard AR-15 with its carry handle and 20-inch barrel made sense but, as it is with most civilians, I'm not in combat.

However, as a police officer, I was one of the designated marksmen for my department. That's an inoffensive way of saying I was a sniper, but a more accurate way of saying I was just one of the best rifle shots in the department. Due to that assignment, I routinely carried one of two rifles in my patrol car. One was a Remington 700 bolt-action rifle in .308, the other a Colt M16 with both semi-auto and full-auto capabilities.

The bolt-action rifle was technically more accurate, but, for about every task I could imagine being called upon where I might need to use a rifle, the M16 would have been my first choice. Officers in my department had been asking for patrol rifles for some time, just as were police officers all across the nation. However, it wasn't until after the North Hollywood bank robbery, where the bad guys

From a tactical application standpoint, no other firearm system is as versatile as the AR.
(Len Waldron photo)

were armed with fully automatic firearms and wearing body armor, that police agencies started to seriously consider patrol rifles.

An AR-style rifle was an obvious choice for police patrol. They are compact, light, accurate, and offer high-volume fire capability. Besides, many agencies were already using one version or another of the AR for their S.W.A.T. teams. Today, the AR is the predominant patrol rifle and, in most cases, it is a semi-auto variant of the M4 carbine the military uses. Many are also equipped with an optical sight of some sort.

Maybe the police application of the AR is best described by Len Waldron, a former U.S. Army Captain currently working as a firearms journalist:

Though plagued by early Vietnam-era troubles largely due to miss-matched ammunition, the modern-day AR is an adaptable platform that operators and LEOs can configure to their specific mission. From Personal Defense Firearms (PDWs) designed to fit under a medium-length garment or to be deployed quickly from inside a vehicle or aircraft, to a heavy-barreled .338 Lapua sniper rifle that can penetrate walls and engine blocks, the core AR platform has been adopted to handle a broad range of loads and projectiles. Additionally, the capacity to add optics, night vision devices, laser targeting systems, and even breaching and indirect fire tools is unmatched. Mission-specific add-ons aside, the AR's fire control ergonomics and buffer spring recoil management system make it a forgiving platform throughout many calibers, applications, and loads. Kept well lubricated and generally clean, a properly configured AR firearm system is a versatile and reliable tool for battle.

As it is with any other firearm adopted on a wholesale basis by law enforcement or the military, civilian interest follows. That, in

Len Waldron has extensive experience with the AR and is frequently involved in testing current and new AR systems and accessories. (Len Waldron photo)

conjunction with the flat-top receiver, which is now more standard than not on toady's ARs, and we see that civilian shooters have fully adopted the AR. But not only have they adopted it, their interest and use of the platform for a variety of endeavors has, to a large extent, driven the manufacture of variations.

In the southern states, where feral hogs are a problem, the AR equipped with night vision devices has become the gun of choice for many.

Hunting with the AR is becoming more and more prevalent, due to the compactness and versatility of the platform. At first, given the small caliber chambering, the AR became a common choice for varmint hunters. Those who like to shoot at prairie dogs and gophers will often shoot hundreds of rounds of ammo in one day. The AR was perfectly suited to this type of shooting and, with a free-floated barrel, will remain accurate even when the barrel heats up. The high-capacity magazines and ability to fire in the semi-automatic mode is also a benefit, because these hunters are often in what might be called a "target rich environment."

Hog hunters were the next group to give the AR a try and, to some extent, for the same reasons varmint hunters were drawn to it. In the southern states, feral hogs are thick to the point they have become a serious nuisance, causing wide-spread crop damage, among other issues. Hunters will often encounter groups of the swine and work

Though it may not look like your daddy's deer rifle, the AR platform is easily adaptable to many types of hunting.

towards more of an eradication exercise than they will actually hunt them, per se. More recently, the use of night vision devices has taken this feral hog eradication into the darkness; with a flat-top rail and a rail extending out on the handguard, it is easy to mount both an optical sight and night vision device on an AR. This applies to both the AR-15 and the AR-10, the latter of which shoots cartridges that are substantially more powerful than the .223 Remington/5.56 NATO.

The threaded muzzle on the AR is also a benefit to hunters who require stealth when attempting to shoot multiple hogs out of a group. I've done this myself on several occasions and was able to shoot as many as five hogs in one group before they figured out where the sound was coming from and which way they needed to run. This may not sound all that sporting, but, keep in mind, going after the feral hog population is no longer considered as much sport as it is an exercise in trying to get a handle on a species that is out of control and destroying farms and crop fields.

Fathers and young shooters are finding that the AR-15, with its lightweight, compact design, and almost non-existent recoil, is the

Suppressors reduce the muzzle blast and report of firearms, and the threaded barrel on the AR makes suppressor installation easy. This is great for young shooters and also protects our hearing.

perfect centerfire starter gun for kids. My son used an AR to take his second deer when he was only seven years old. The collapsible stock fit him perfectly and, in fact, can grow with a kid as they do.

If you are looking for an opinion from someone who is intimately familiar with modern firearms suitable for use in a variety of situations, Adam Heggenstaller, Editor in Chief for the National Rifle Association's *Shooting Illustrated* magazine, is a good one to listen to. Not only has Heggenstaller used the AR in many situations and he is a very experienced hunter. By virtue of his position, he gets to experiment with most of the modern and even some antiquated firearms available. Here's what he had to say about the AR:

Adam Heggenstaller has extensive experience with all modern firearm systems and is also an accomplished hunter. (Adam Heggenstaller photo)

The AR platform has three major things going for it that make it suitable for a variety of tasks: a semi-automatic action, a detachable box magazine, and modularity unequaled by any other firearm design. Whether defending your home or taking a follow-up shot at a whitetail, having another bullet ready to immediately send toward the target is an undeniable advantage. Thanks to detachable box magazines of varying length and capacity, you can load the AR with anywhere from five to 100 rounds to fit the

situation. If there's some feature you want to change to tailor the gun for a specific use, a long list of options exists for just about every component, most of which you can drop in right at home. With the possible exception of dangerous-game hunting, I can't think of anything an AR will not do.

Shooters have also found that shooting an AR is fun, just as they've discovered the enjoyment to be had in building and accessorizing them. Unlike other long guns, the AR is infinitely customizable. There are accessories and gadgets that can be attached in all manner to the AR, something you will not find for any other firearm. Some have even termed the AR as the adult version of the Lego.

Since the modern firearm has become readily available to American citizens, the AR marks the first time a shooter could buy his gun in parts and assemble it on his own with-

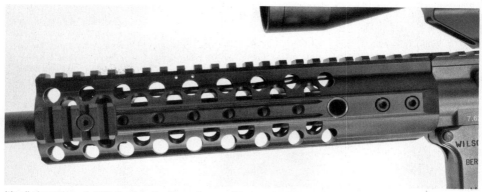

It's all about the rail. With the free-floating rail on an AR, the possibilities are almost endless.

out any expensive tools or serious training. This has a great deal of appeal to gun owners who have always dreamed of building their own rifle. Not only that, the cartridge an AR-10 or AR-15 fires can be changed in seconds by simply switching the upper receiver (and that operation only requires the pushing out of two pins). Now shooters could have a switch-barrel rifle, something that before the AR was only possible with single-shot rifles or very expensive custom bolt-action rifles.

Just as it is with men who are passionate about accessorizing their cars, trucks, bass boats, and 4x4s, with the AR, they could now do the same types of things with their rifle. Maybe even to a greater extent. Say you have a basic AR and you want to hunt deer.

No problem. Maybe you want to use it for home-defense. No problem. What if you want to compete in shooting matches, both tactical and long-range? No problem. There are AR accessories that will allow you to make these conversions on your own, and you can go back and forth as your heart desires.

Competition with the AR, just like with hunting, has created an entire industry of ARs and AR accessories. Since 2010, 3-Gun competition has become the fastest growing shooting sport in America. In 3-Gun, shooters need a handgun, a shotgun, and some sort of semi-automatic rifle. (In some stages, the contestants will shoot all three firearms, while in others just one or two.) The AR is the dominant rifle is this sport, without question.

With one AR, you can do a lot of things. You can have one upper for personal protection, one for varmints, and one for big-game hunting.

3-Gun competition is dominated by the AR and puts shooters in wildly exciting and challenging shooting situations. *The 14th Reinstated* author Bryce Towsley is an avid 3-Gun shooter. (Bryce Towsley photo)

In the sport of 3-Gun, the distances to the targets intended to be engaged with the AR can vary from as close as a few feet on out to several hundred yards. This means that competitors need to set up their ARs for shooting near and far, and specialized sighting systems and even cartridges have been developed to maximize the competitive advantage the platform offers.

Bryce Towsley has probably written about and fired more firearms than any gun writer currently working. He's hunted all over the world and is an avid 3-Gun competitor. Towsley can shoot, too, I've seen it firsthand. Though long a fixture with the gun crowd, Towsley recently entered the world of fiction writing, with his novel, *The 14th Reinstated*. This book, which details the social and economic collapse of the free world, specifically highlights the suitability of the AR as an end-of-days survival tool. I asked Towsley about his book and the AR:

If social collapse occurs, it will be up to you to take responsibility for your safety and the safety of your family. You cannot depend on society, the police, the rule of law, or the government to help you. You are on your own.

Bryce Towsley has tested and reported on thousands of firearms throughout his gun writing career. When he chose to write a book, *The 14th Reinstated*, a novel about economic and social collapse, his hero was armed with an AR. (Bryce Towsley photo)

As illustrated in my novel, The 14th Reinstated, *trying to defend your home against an angry mob with your hunting guns will not work. The guns don't hold enough ammo and are much too slow to reload. You will be overrun as soon as you pause to reload. The only acceptable civilian-owned firearm for this situation is a magazine-fed rifle or carbine. The best of the best is the AR-15 platform. It is the most common design in America, so magazines, ammo, and parts are easily available. It's also the fastest to operate. A well-trained shooter can reload his AR in about one second.*

The 5.56 is a NATO cartridge, so ammo is probably going to be available no matter how bad it gets. The gun can also fire .223 Remington, which is one of the most common cartridges in North America.

The AR is a battle rifle and, so, is designed for a high, sustained rate of fire. They run hot and will just keep puking out the ammo no matter what. Most are extremely accurate for handling long-range targets, while also fast for addressing multiple-target close-range engagements.

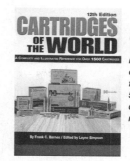

Cartridges of the World, 13th Edition lists many new AR-compatible cartridges. This is the first time in the volume's 50-year history that AR cartridges dominated the newest entries.

There seems to be no end in sight, with regards to the research and development of AR accessories and cartridges. I recently edited *Cartridges of the World, 13th Edition*, a book that has been the bible for cartridges for almost 50 years. Part of my job editing that volume was to identify new commercial and wildcat cartridges. The new cartridges in the *13th Edition* were predominately for the AR platform and that's the first time this could be said since the original edition was published, in 1965!

For the exact same reasons people gravitate to smart phones, they are becoming AR aficionados. It's simple, really: no other rifle offers as much for as little. You can own one AR-15 and fire cartridges as small as the .22 LR and as large as the .50 Beowulf. You can use an AR-15 or an AR-10 and hunt every species of game on the North American continent. You can equip an AR for short-range defensive shooting, for long-range target

Whether you are hunting or just trying to survive, the AR platform offers more versatility than any other firearm system.

The AR is the one-gun answer.

shooting, for high-volume varmint shooting, for shooting at night, and for shooting suppressed ammo. And you can do all of this with the same rifle.

It wasn't all that long ago you could have described a rifle like this to some firearms expert and they would have told you that it does not and could not exist. Now, if there is a limit to what you can do with the AR, it is imposed not by the characteristics of the firearm platform, but by legislation. And that is an ever-evolving subject that, in today's climate seems to be changing by the minute rather than by the day, month, or year.

Maybe the most spectacular thing about the AR is that it is more than 50 years old and yet is still one of the most *modern* firearms available. It also seems that the older the AR gets, the more uses we find for it and the more shooters there are who fall in love with it. As a gun owner, it's nice to have a rifle set up perfectly for a specific task. The AR is the only rifle that allows you to do this and have one rifle that's perfectly suited for

multiple tasks. Sure, you might have to turn a screw or flip a lever to make that transition, but that's what versatility is in the modern world.

Interestingly, as comprehensive as this book tries to be at introducing shooters to the AR, it cannot be complete. This is because the AR and the accessories for it are evolving as fast as gadgets in the computer and smartphone worlds. Never before has this type of continued advancement and evolution occurred so rapidly with any other firearms system. To date, there has simply been nothing like the AR. It can be the one gun you own that will do almost anything you need it to do. Maybe that's why some of the anti-gun crowd is so firmly against the AR. It's no secret they would like to limit the number of firearms we own, if they cannot succeed in taking them all. The AR represents a challenge to the notion that the citizenry would be less controllable or potentially dangerous to a rouge government if they had only one gun.

CHAPTER 3

THE AR-10 AND THE AR-15

When shooters who have no experience with an AR look at it, they can, at best, often feel some intimidation. At worst, their eyes glass over and their pulse rises. This is primarily because the AR does not look like your "traditional" rifle. This is really not a big deal. An iPhone looks nothing like those rotary phones we used when I was growing up, nor even anything like the cell phones we were using just 15 years ago.

Yes, the AR looks different and that can be the source of some apprehension, but the truth is, it is, in fact, a very uncomplicated rifle, which is partly why it looks as it does. Simply described, it is made up of a lower receiver, which contains the trigger group and the magazine well. The

ARs come in a variety of configurations, but the basic parts are all the same.

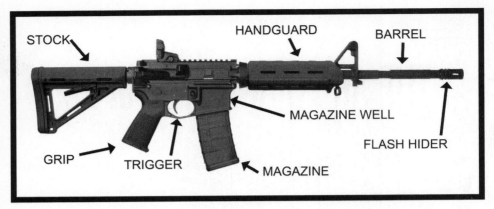

STOCK HANDGUARD BARREL

MAGAZINE WELL

FLASH HIDER

GRIP TRIGGER MAGAZINE

Major parts of the AR.

stock is also attached to the lower receiver. The upper receiver houses the bolt and is connected to the barrel and the gas system that makes the gun work. That's really all there is to it. However, just as it is with a chainsaw or any other mechanical tool, to be comfortable with a machine, you need to understand all the controls and how they function, both individually and as a system.

Let's sort out the parts inside and out, and then we'll examine how the AR-15 and AR-10 work. By breaking the AR down into the two main parts of the upper and lower receiver, it's easier to comprehend the overall system and make it easier to understand how these two pieces work together to make the AR function and provide the versatility it offers. (Note: While an AR-15 and an AR-10 are quite a bit different in size, their parts—though most are not interchangeable—are very similar in shape and practically identical in their intended functionality.)

THE LOWER RECEIVER

The lower receiver of an AR is manufactured of aluminum. This is the serial numbered part

of an AR and is the part that must be put on a BATFE (Bureau of Alcohol, Tobacco, Firearms and Explosives) Form 4473, when an AR is purchased. In other words, this is the only AR part that is controlled by the federal government. If you purchase an AR, the serial number from the lower receiver is recorded. If you purchase *just* a lower receiver for an AR, the same thing happens. (There is also a federal regulation that stipulates a minimum barrel length of 16 inches on any rifle. While the barrel purchase in and of itself is not something that is controlled, if a barrel shorter than 16 inches is *attached* to any shoulder-

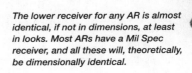

The lower receiver for any AR is almost identical, if not in dimensions, at least in looks. Most ARs have a Mil Spec receiver, and all these will, theoretically, be dimensionally identical.

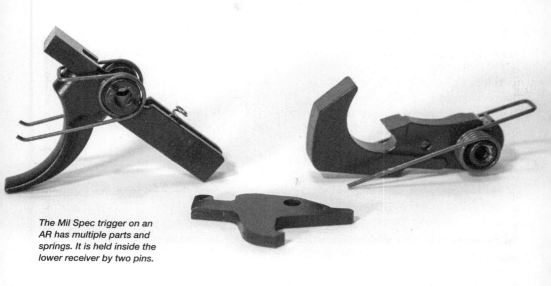

The Mil Spec trigger on an AR has multiple parts and springs. It is held inside the lower receiver by two pins.

fired rifle, including an AR, certain other federal regulations have to be met.)

The stock and pistol grip are attached to this lower receiver, and inside you'll find the trigger group. There are three controls on the lower receiver; the safety selector switch, the bolt stop/release, and the magazine release. The only other part of the lower receiver of any real importance is the magazine well, which is where you insert the magazine that can contain as few as five rounds or as many as 100, depending upon its design.

THE TRIGGER GROUP

Like all other firearms, the AR has a trigger. This is the lever you pull to make the AR go bang. The trigger assembly is held in place inside the lower receiver by two pins; if you look on the lower receiver of any AR, these two pins are visible just above the trigger, on both sides. A factory Mil Spec trigger on an AR is made of a variety of parts and is somewhat difficult to assemble if you are unfamiliar with the system. If you are not familiar with how an AR trigger works, don't screw around with it.

THE LOWER RECEIVER CONTROLS

The safety selector switch on a semi-automatic AR has two positions, SAFE and FIRE. In the SAFE position, the switch is

The safety selector switch is on the left side of the lower receiver. Some ARs come with an ambidextrous safety selector switch.

The bolt stop/release can be used to lock the bolt to the rear or release the bolt and allow it to move forward into battery.

positioned parallel to the barrel. In the FIRE position, the switch is in the up position, perpendicular to the barrel. Some lower receivers may also have engraving showing a third position for fully automatic or three-round burst fire. This is because the same company might also manufacturer full-auto ARs for the military or law enforcement. If you have an AR and the safety selection switch can be moved to this third position and you do not have permission from the BATFE (better known as the ATF) to own a full-auto firearm, you have a problem.

On the left side of the lower receiver, the same side of the receiver where you will find the safety selector switch, you will see the bolt stop/release. It is positioned in the center of the receiver, just above the trigger and immediately behind the magazine well. This control serves several purposes. It allows you to lock the bolt to the rear and it will also automatically lock the bolt to the rear after

the last round in the magazine has been fired. Finally, this control also allows you to release the bolt, so it can go forward and into battery.

The third and final control on the lower receiver is the magazine release. It is located on the right side, just above the front of the trigger guard. By pushing the magazine release, you are able to release the magazine from the lower receiver.

THE STOCK

At the rear top of the lower receiver there is a circular projection that is threaded on the inside. This is how the stock is attached to the AR. Once the stock is threaded in place, there is a jam nut that secures the stock.

Standard AR stocks are hollow, though there is a cylindrical tube within the stock where the buffer and buffer spring are housed. If you are familiar with semi-automatic rifles and handguns, you might call this the recoil spring. When the AR is fired, this recoil spring

The magazine release is positioned just forward of the trigger at the edge of the magazine well. When pushed, it allows the magazine to drop free of the AR.

Magazines for the AR vary from those that hold five cartridges to others that can hold as many as 100.

This is a collapsible buttstock for an AR that allows the shooter to adjust it to best fit them or a particular situation. Several versions of the collapsible buttstock are available.

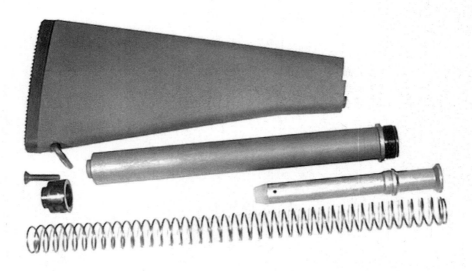

Regardless the type of stock used on an AR, it will contain a buffer tube, buffer, and a buffer spring.

is compacted and it then pushes the bolt forward, loading the next cartridge as it goes. The recoil spring and buffer are held in place by a spring-loaded button called the "buffer retainer," which is positioned at the bottom of the circular, threaded projection.

THE GRIP

The grip on the AR should be obvious. It is located at the bottom rear of the lower receiver and is held in place by a single screw. The grip on an AR is easy to change out, and doing so is a very common upgrade. However, take note that the grip also holds a small spring and plunger in place, collectively called the "safety detent." This very small part is what maintains pressure on the safety lever, allowing it to work. If you happen to decide to replace the grip on the lower receiver of your AR, be careful not to lose this.

THE TAKEDOWN PINS

At the front and rear of the lower receiver there are two pins. These are the takedown pins, and they serve the purpose of holding the upper and lower receivers together. It is these two pins that are the keys to the modularity of the AR platform. In seconds, you can pull these pins (which are held captive in the lower receiver), remove your upper receiver, and position another upper receiver

There are many types of grips for an AR, but they all serve the same purpose, which is to provide something for your shooting hand to hold on to.

in place. When you push the two pins back in, they will lock the new upper receiver onto the lower receiver. These two pins are also the key to disassembling the AR.

THE UPPER RECEIVER

The upper receiver of an AR is also made of aluminum. It is held in place, on top of the

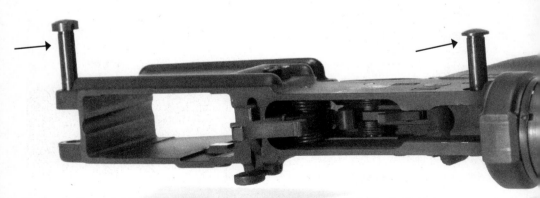

The heart of the modularity of the AR platform lies in the takedown pins, which allow fast and easy access to the internals of the gun, as well as the ability to switch uppers and change the configuration.

The upper receiver of the AR contains the bolt and is what the barrel is attached to.

lower receiver, by the two takedown pins. The upper receiver houses the bolt group that contains the bolt and the firing pin. It is also what the barrel is attached to. Some upper receivers have an integral carry handle like the original AR-15/M16. Others will have a section of Picatinny/Mil Spec rail along the top to which a rear sight, a carry handle with an integral rear sight, or an optical sight can be attached. The barrel and the handguard attach to the front of the upper receiver and, as it is with the lower receiver, there are three controls on the upper receiver.

THE UPPER RECEIVER CONTROLS

At the top rear of the upper receiver you will find the charging handle. This handle allows you to pull the bolt group, which is inside the upper receiver, to the rear. This compresses the buffer spring inside the stock and, when you release the charging handle,

the bolt and charging handle both move forward. Alternately, you can use the charging handle to retract the bolt and then lock it in the retracted position by using the bolt stop/release. If you do this, you will then need to push the charging handle forward and lock it back into place. The charging handle allows you to operate the bolt, but the charging handle does not operate with the bolt when the AR is being fired.

Mil Spec ARs, those designed to meet military specifications, will have a control that is called a "forward assist." The forward assist was incorporated into the design to allow solders to have a way to push the bolt forward during combat, if the rifle's insides became dirty from excessive firing or due to the environmental conditions. When you push on the forward assist, it applies pressure to a partially closed bolt and helps it move into the fully closed position, "into battery," as some

The charging handle in the forward position (left). When pulled to the rear (right), the charging handle retracts the bolt, as you can see here with the upper receiver separated from the lower receiver.

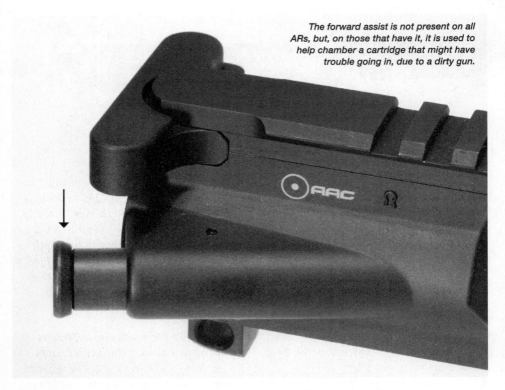

The forward assist is not present on all ARs, but, on those that have it, it is used to help chamber a cartridge that might have trouble going in, due to a dirty gun.

like to call it. Some very modern ARs lack a forward assist now. The platform has become so reliable that it rarely if ever fails to fully chamber a cartridge, especially when using good-quality factory ammunition.

The dust cover is another design element of the original AR that is sometimes no longer carried over to modern ARs. It was put in place to help keep dirt and crud out of the inside of the upper receiver, when the AR wasn't being fired. It has application in battlefield conditions, not so much so for the civilian shooter. Once you have loaded your AR, you can close the dust cover and it will latch in place, providing a shield to the bolt group and the inside of the upper receiver against outside contaminates. When you fire the AR, the dust cover automatically opens and will remain open until you manually close it.

The dust cover is designed to keep debris and dirt out of the AR's action, when it is not being fired. Not all modern ARs have a dust cover anymore.

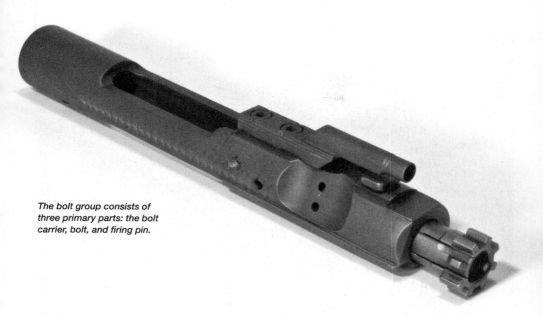

The bolt group consists of three primary parts: the bolt carrier, bolt, and firing pin.

THE BOLT GROUP

The AR bolt group has three primary parts: the bolt carrier, the bolt, and the firing pin. The bolt carrier houses both the bolt and the firing pin and is the component that cycles back and forth inside the upper receiver as the AR is being fired. The bolt is located at the front of the bolt carrier, and it rotates and moves forwards and backwards inside the bolt carrier. The bolt also contains the extractor, which pulls cartridge cases from the chamber of the AR, and the ejector, which forces the cartridge cases out through the ejection port. The firing pin is inserted into the rear of the bolt and, when the hammer strikes it, it will protrude through the end of the bolt face.

THE BARREL

The AR's barrel is attached to the front of the upper receiver and is held in place by a large threaded nut. The most common barrel on an AR is a 16-inch carbine barrel. However, a variety of barrel lengths are available, and these barrels will have a variety of rifling twist rates. As it is with any rifle, you can also have heavy barrels, fluted barrels, and barrels with a range of tapers and thicknesses.

THE HANDGUARD

Probably the second-most common upgrade shooters make to their ARs is the installation of an aftermarket handguard. The varieties seem as endless as the types of shoes you could wear. In fact, shoes are

AR barrels vary in style, and in length ranging from 16 to 24 inches. They can be changed, though this is a task generally best accomplished by a gunsmith or someone with experience working with ARs. Barrels shorter than 16 inches and, when installed on an AR (with the proper paperwork and ATF tax stamps for civilian use), the AR is then known as an "SBR," or "short barreled rifle."

Handguards on the AR can be changed to allow the configuration you desire. They are probably the second-most common AR upgrade made by shooters. The handguard on this AR is the once very common two-piece military style.

a great comparison to handguards, because you select different shoes based on what you want to do. Same with a handguard.

The most common handguard is the two-piece military style, which is held in place by a spring-loaded collar. The free-floating handguards, which might be smooth or covered with various short or full sections of Picatinny or Mil Spec rail, are threaded onto the front of the upper receiver. The handguard, regardless its style, attaches to the outside of the barrel nut and covers the barrel and all or part of the gas system.

THE GAS SYSTEM

The gas produced while the gunpowder inside the cartridge case is burning is what makes an AR work. In order for this gas to do the job it needs to, it needs to be controlled and directed to the right place.

At a point along the top of an AR's barrel there is a hole. As gas follows the bullet

down the barrel, it leaks into this hole and into what is called the "gas block." The gas block then diverts the gas into a tube, which runs back to and inside of the upper receiver. At the end of this tube, the gas exits and pushes against the "gas key," which is located on top of the bolt carrier. This push of gas forces the bolt carrier to the rear.

Some gas blocks are adjustable. This allows the shooter to sort of tune their AR much as you would time a car engine. This can be helpful when different types of ammo are used and is especially important when shooting with a suppressor or with subsonic ammunition. By tuning the flow of gas, you can control the functioning or timing of the AR.

THE MUZZLE

The end of the barrel on most ARs is threaded. This is done primarily for the attachment of a flash hider, which is that

GAS TUBE   GAS BLOCK

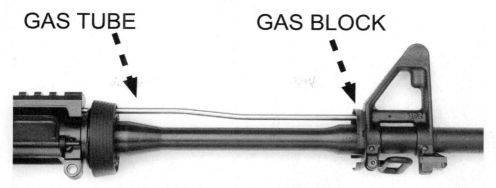

The gas system on the AR is what makes it work. Gas is funneled from the barrel, through the tube, and back into the upper receiver. (Oleg Volk photo)

GAS KEY

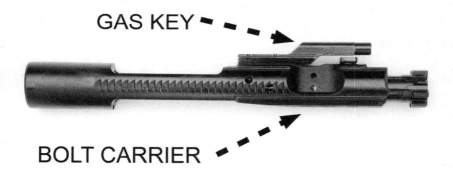

BOLT CARRIER

A gas key is positioned on top of the bolt carrier. This is where the gas from the inside of the barrel is diverted to via the gas block and gas tube. (Oleg Volk photo)

birdcage-looking thing you see on the end of most every AR barrel.

A flash hider serves two primary purposes. First, it protects the crown of the barrel so that the rifling, which is exposed at the muzzle, does not become damaged. If the crown is damaged, accuracy will suffer. The flash hider also limits the visual signature seen when the AR is fired. In a combat or law enforcement situation, this makes the muzzle blast of the AR harder to see and, so, the location of the shooter behind it harder to pinpoint.

AR muzzles are also threaded so that a suppressor can be attached. Like a flash hider, a sound suppressor screws onto the end of the barrel. Such a tool limits the audible signature when the AR is fired.

THE PARTS AS A WHOLE

Now that you know about the most important parts of your AR, it's time to see how they all work together to make the gun function.

When you retract the charging handle of an AR and lock the bolt to the rear by depressing the bolt stop/release, you have, essentially, cocked the firing system. As the bolt is drawn to the rear, it pushes down on the hammer, which pivots on a pin. As the bolt slides over the hammer, a projection of the hammer is pushed in between a "C"-like opening on the trigger. At the front of the "C," a hook on the trigger captures the hammer and holds it in place in the cocked position.

With a loaded magazine inserted into the magazine well, the bolt stop/release can be

Most ARs have a threaded muzzle and come with a flash hider, and there are a tremendous number of design variations. Some flash hiders even work as compensators, to reduce recoil. Threaded muzzles can also accept suppressors.

depressed. Doing so releases the bolt, which will move forward and push a cartridge from the magazine into the barrel's chamber. The force of the bolt moving forward causes the lugs on the bolt face to engage the recess in the end of the barrel, and the bolt will lock into battery. This same force allows the extractor, which is positioned on the outer edge of the bolt face, to slip over the rim of the cartridge case.

If the safety selector switch is placed in the FIRE position and the trigger is pulled, the hammer will be released, pivoting forward, because it is under spring tension. The hammer will move through the opening in the bottom of the bolt carrier and the face of the hammer will strike the end of the firing pin that is under spring tension. The impact of the hammer will drive the firing pin forward through the bolt face until it strikes the primer of the cartridge that is in the chamber.

Once struck, the explosive material inside the primer rapidly burns, and the flame passes through the hole at the base of the cartridge case and ignites the gunpowder within the cartridge case. As this gunpowder burns, it creates high volumes of gas. The pressure associated with this gas forces the bullet out of the cartridge case. The case then very slightly expands and locks itself inside the barrel's chamber. As the bullet passes down the barrel, the gas follows and the pressure is maintained behind the bullet until the bullet exits the barrel.

When the bullet passes the hole in the barrel we talked about under the heading "The Gas System," that hole positioned on the top of the barrel and which is covered by the gas block, a small amount of the gas escapes through this hole and into the gas block, where it is directed into the gas tube. The gas, still under pressure, passes through the gas tube and is directed into the gas key, which is positioned on top of the bolt carrier. The pressure here is high enough to push the bolt carrier to the rear and compress the buffer spring, which is housed inside the AR's stock. As the bolt carrier moves to the rear, the bolt starts to rotate. This happens just about at the exact time the cartridge case has shrunk back to its normal size—the expansion I spoke about is a temporary condition and demonstrates the fluidity and elasticity of cartridge case material—and, so, the brass releases itself from the barrel's chamber.

As the bolt continuous its reward motion, the extractor on the bolt, which, as you'll remember, is clipped over the rim of the cartridge case, now pulls the cartridge from the chamber. The bolt carrier and bolt continue their reward travel, which also pulls the fired cartridge case to the rear. At the same time, the ejector, which is a spring-loaded plunger in the bolt's face, is pushing against the cartridge case and, as the mouth of the cartridge case clears the ejection port, the ejector pushes the case out of the upper receiver. This push is sort of like a flip, since the rim of the cartridge case opposite the ejector is still trapped under the extractor. At this point, the bolt carrier and bolt have just about reached the limit of their reward motion and, once again, the bolt carrier has forced the projection on the back of the hammer down into the "C"-like opening on the top of the trigger bar.

All of this has happened before the shooter can release their pressure on the trigger. Because of the speed in this process, the notch at the front of the "C" opening cannot capture the hammer as it did on the initial cocking, so now a notch on the rear section of the "C" opening grabs the hammer and holds it in place.

All the pressurized gas is now out of the AR and the buffer, under the pressure of the buffer spring, begins pushing the bolt carrier forward. As it does so, the bolt pushes another cartridge up and out of the magazine and into the chamber of the barrel. By now the shooter has released the pressure on the trigger, and the notch on the rear of the "C" opening releases the hammer but, now the notch on the front of this "C" opening captures the hammer and the AR is once again cocked and ready to be fired again. This entire procedure continues until the shooter stops firing and either decides to unload the AR or until all the ammunition inside the magazine has been expended. Once this latter happens, the follower in the magazine pushes against the bolt stop, which serves to lock the bolt to the rear.

All this may seem a bit complex, so allow me to simplify. When a cartridge is fired in an AR, the gas that is generated is used to cycle the action and chamber a new cartridge. This is why the AR is often called a "gas gun"—it runs off gas. Not liquid gas or gasoline like your Corvette uses, but the formless gas generated by the burning gunpowder inside the cartridge case.

Modern ARs will run this cycle time and time again, maybe even a thousand or more times, before you run into any problems. Those problems, when they do happen, come from the carbon deposits or carbon fouling the burning gas leaves inside the gun's mechanism.

This gassing of the mechanism or, as some shooters call it, "pooping where it eats," is considered a problem and is why we now have ARs that are driven by a piston.

CHAPTER 4

GAS IMPINGEMENT VERSUS GAS PISTON

As described in the pervious chapter, the original AR, as designed by Eugene Stoner, functions on the gas impingement system. To recap, as the bullet travels down the barrel, it passes a hole in the top of the barrel and a small amount of the gas pushing the bullet is diverted through this hole. The gas is then directed back through a tube and into the upper receiver, where it pushes against the gas key on top of the bolt carrier. This pushes the bolt carrier back and cycles the action.

There are three complaints with this system. The first is that this dispersion of hot gas into the receiver heats up the operating components of the AR. Hey, this gas is very hot, a lot hotter than the empty cases that are ejected. During sustained fire, this can create a lot of heat, and this heat can, theoreti-cally, cause additional wear to the operating components. The heat also bakes the carbon residue contained in the powder onto the bolt and bolt carrier. The third complaint is the fouling. Regardless how hot you get your AR, all that carbon fouling is still deposited inside the operating mechanism.

Some correlate this gas impingement operating system to a person who poops on the same table they eat off of. I have no idea where they get the statistical or scientific data to support this analogy, but the premise is that a gas impingement-driven AR throws all its waste (carbon fouling) right into the same area where it eats, operates, and feeds its new ammo inside the action.

First off, and before we get into the gas piston system, let's look at whether this is

IMPINGEMENT GAS SYSTEM

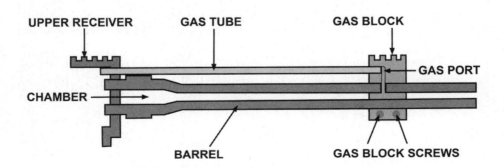

With the gas impingement system, gas is diverted from the barrel through a tube and back into the upper receiver to operate the action.

Though ARs come in all shapes and sizes, there are primarily two distinct operating systems the platform employs, gas impingement and gas piston. To the untrained eye, they are almost indistinguishable.

a real problem. Yes, you can shoot a gas impingement AR enough that it will become fouled to the point it will not operate reliably. The problem is I cannot tell you how much shooting this will require. It depends on the amount of carbon deposits produced by the ammo, and that varies from ammo to ammo. It also depends on how hot you get your AR while you're shooting it.

I have a Smith & Wesson M&P 15 I've owned for six years. I have shot it thousands of times. I have never, ever cleaned it and I have never lubed it. However, I have never fired more than a magazine (30 rounds) at a time. In other words I have never gotten the rifle really hot. Additionally, I have taken a variety of carbine training courses in which I fired between 500 and 1,000 rounds of ammo over several days and, yes, some of

those guns got really hot and really dirty. I didn't clean them either, nor did I have a single functioning issue.

On the other hand, I have tested a variety of ARs from many manufacturers, using a wide variety of ammo, and, on occasion, I've run into functioning problems that were corrected by cleaning the AR, sometimes after as few as 200 rounds. For what it's worth, this might be a good place to add that the No. 1 cause of malfunctioning issues with an AR has nothing to do with fouling, but is most often caused by faulty magazines. In fact, this is generally the cause of malfunctioning problems with any semi-auto firearm. Bottom line is, though, if you are in combat or fighting zombies and you're shooting thousands of rounds per day without any opportunity to clean your AR,

The AK is a fully automatic battle rifle that operates on the gas piston principle. It is extremely reliable.

particularly if you are shooting at a fast rate of fire and getting the AR very hot, you may very well run into a situation where the heat and fouling does cause functioning issues that can only be corrected by lots of lubrication or a judicious cleaning.

This might be a good time to interject something else. Just because an AR is a mechanical device does not mean you need to soak it in lubrication. Indeed, lubrication can make the moving parts move and work together easier, but soaking the internals of an AR can cause a dangerous situation. If you get excess lubrication in the chamber and bore of the AR, you can create an overpressure situation that can have disastrous consequences. A little lube goes a long way on an AR, especially if it is applied to the right spots. (For more on lubrication and cleaning, check out Chapter 10, which covers AR maintenance.)

But back to the topic at hand, and that is which operating system might be best for the AR. One of the most reliable battle rifles of all time is the AK-47, which was designed by Mikhail Kalashnikov. Like the AR, the AK runs on gas, but, instead of using direct gas to operate the action, the AK uses the gas to drive a piston/rod attached to the bolt carrier. This rod essentially does what the gas in a gas-operated AR does and pushes the bolt carrier to the rear, cycling the action. The gas in the AK is then vented to the outside and, so, never enters the action area of the rifle.

In addition to having a great reputation for reliability, the AK also has an equally bad reputation for inaccuracy. In close quarters this isn't an issue, but, if you are trying to hit a man-sized target or something smaller at several hundred yards with an AK, all I'll say is good luck.

There are a variety of reasons the AK is not very accurate, and one of those is the piston operating system. You see, this piston induces barrel torque. It also negatively impacts barrel harmonics. At the same time, due to its piston operating system, the AK runs much cooler and cleaner than the AR, because none of those hot gases are making their way back into the action. This led some designers to consider the possibility of making an AR that would run with a piston system. Some called this an attempt to solve a problem that didn't exist, while others saw it as the second coming of John Browning.

With a piston-driven AR, when the gas enters the gas block, it is used to force a

GAS PISTON SYSTEM

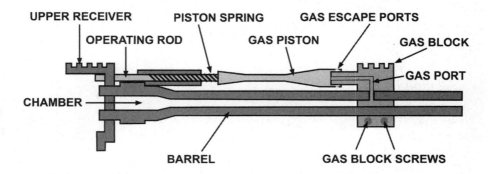

With the gas piston system, gas is funneled from the barrel to drive a piston that works the action.

piston or rod back against what is called the gas key on a gas impingement AR. On a piston-driven AR, however, this gas key does not have a hole in it. Instead, it is just a solid block for the piston to pound against.

On the positive side, all the gas is expunged from the system at the gas block, so the internals of a piston-driven AR stay very clean and quite cool. On the negative side, the bolt carrier inside an AR was not designed to be pounded on with a steel rod, and this pounding at the front end of the bolt carrier causes the bolt carrier to tilt as is functions. Theoretically, this induces undue wear on the upper receiver and bolt carrier. Also theoretically, the operating rod system makes the rifle less accurate, because its connection to the barrel can influence torque as the barrel heats, thereby interfering with barrel harmonicas as the bullet travels down its length. Finally, the impulse of the piston slapping the bolt carrier changes the way the rifle feels when it recoils. Recoil is intensified in this case, though admittedly to such a slight degree that most shooters will not be able to discern it.

Though it has nothing to do with the operation of the AR, there is one other downside to the piston-driven design: it costs more. Many piston-driven ARs cost twice as much as most gas impingement ARs. So, maybe the real question is, is the piston-driven system worth the money?

I asked the only super soldier I know about his thoughts on the gas impingement versus piston question. Cody Carroll works for Magpul in product development and research and has been over in the sand box as a solider and a sniper for the Army and the Marines. In short, he has pulled a lot of AR triggers when it really mattered. Cody told me, "My thoughts are the gas system works best on mid- and rifle-length guns, but, if you want a carbine or PDW (Personal Defense Weapon), you need a piston. The HK416, for instance, is a tank. I'd trade all of my gas guns for the reliability and life-span of the 416."

The bolt carrier on top is the type used with the gas impingement system. With it, gas enters the key and pushes the bolt carrier to the rear. The bottom bolt carrier is the type used with the gas piston design. The key on this bolt carrier is smaller and is impacted by the piston that is pushed to the rear by gas. (Oleg Volk photo)

Here are the two operating systems exposed. On the top is the gas impingement system and on the bottom the piston system. Both can vary in length—the distance from the action to the gas block—and some theorize that this length is a determining factor regarding which system is best. (Oleg Volk photo)

Just so you know, the HK416 is a weapon system designed and manufactured by Heckler & Koch. It uses the AR-15 platform and was conceived to be an improvement to the Colt M4 carbine currently issued to the U.S. military, but with the notable inclusion of an HK-proprietary short-stroke gas piston system derived from the Heckler & Koch G36. Considering Cody's background, his opinion is worth listening to.

His comments also bring up another point that needs addressing. Cody mentioned the mid- and rifle-length gas systems. What he is referring to is the fact that the gas system for ARs can vary in length. Usually, the length of the barrel dictates the length of the gas system, and there are primarily four different gas system lengths for an AR: pistol-, carbine-, mid-, and rifle-length.

Pistol-length gas systems are used on AR pistols or what is often called a PDW, which have barrels of 10 inches or less in length. A pistol-length gas tube is only about 4.5 inches long. Carbine-length gas tubes are most commonly found on ARs with barrels between 10 and 18 inches in length. With a

carbine-length gas system, the gas tube is about seven inches long. This is the most common gas system in use on ARs today. Mid-length gas systems are used on ARs with barrels between 14 and 20 inches long. The gas tube for a mid-length system will be around 9.5 inches long. With a rifle-length gas system, the gas tube is about a foot long, and such a tube is most commonly found on ARs with barrels 20 inches or longer.

The general consensus is that the longer the gas system (gas tube), the less wear and tear that will be experienced on the upper receiver. Too, the longer the gas tube, the longer the handguard design that can be used, too. This is because the handguard generally runs out only as far as the gas block on the barrel. Recently, low-profile gas blocks are becoming more popular; they fit low enough to the barrel that the handguard can extend out beyond the gas block. This works very well and will allow you to increase your sight radius and mount other devices like night vision optics on your AR. Still, if you want the versatility of the adjustable gas block, you have to have access to it.

An adjustable gas block provides more versatility for the AR. It allows you to tune the system for use with subsonic ammo, with a suppressor, or over a variety of ammunition.

In that case, it will need to be exposed, and that means the handguard must stop short of the gas block. Decisions, decisions. Your only option, if you have an AR and want to change the length of the gas system, is to purchase a new barrel and gas system. Or, obviously, you could go with a different, complete upper receiver that has a different length gas system. One thing's for sure: with an AR, you'll run out of money before you run out of options.

Ultimately, it's a call only you can make. I can only offer my opinion based on firsthand experience. As someone who tests and reviews guns for a variety of firearms periodicals, I've had the opportunity to test versions of both the gas impingement and piston-driven ARs. Here are my factual discoveries:

1. Piston-driven guns run much cleaner. Fire a 30-round magazine through a piston-driven AR and it will look just as clean afterwards as it did before you fired it.
2. Piston-driven guns run much cooler. You'll have to shoot about 100 rounds through a piston gun and a gas gun to really feel the difference, but it is there.
3. On average, piston-driven guns are less accurate. This does not mean piston-driven ARs are *in*accurate, but, looking over my test records, the most accurate ARs I've tested have been those that work with the gas impingement system.
4. On average, piston-driven guns cost more. This observation must be qualified with "it depends." There are some very expensive gas impinge-ment ARs and some piston-driven ARs that are not all that expensive. However, if you want to purchase the least expensive AR possible, it will be a gas impingement gun.
5. If you intend to run a suppressor on your AR, it has been my experience that the gas impingement guns are more suppressor-friendly, especially those with an adjustable gas block that allows you to control the amount of gas directed back through the gas tube.
6. Both piston-driven and gas impinge-ment guns are very reliable. If, by magic, you inserted me in the pages of Bryce Towsley's book *The 14th Reinstated* and I had to live through a social and economic collapse where there were roving bands of marauders, and if you told me I had to pick between a gas impingement or a piston-driven AR, I really would not care which one I ended up with. Except for three things: parts for gas impingement ARs are easier to find, much more plentiful, and less expensive.

Now, here's the good news. The un-matched modularity of the AR allows you to, in a way, have your cake and eat it, too. If you own a gas impingement AR and want to try a piston-driven AR, just purchase a piston-driven upper receiver. Since the gas impingement and piston systems work independently of the lower receiver, you can alternate between both on the same lower receiver.

An alternate upper receiver can be had for about half the price of a complete AR and you can swap one with your current upper receive in, oh, about 10 seconds. If you want to use your AR for high-volume competition or fun on the range, maybe you should opt for a piston-driven upper receiver to use during those range sessions. Then you could have another upper that is gas driven, if you are shooting less volume or where accuracy is a premium.

I've said it before in this book and I'll say it gain later on. Heck, I'm not sure it can be said too many times. The AR is the most adaptable and versatile rifle in existence. No other firearms platform offers you as many options or will allow you to swap between different operating system with as much ease as the AR. So, if you cannot decide between a gas impingement and a piston AR, get both, shoot them both, and find out for yourself if the piston is an answer to a problem that never existed.

CHAPTER 5

CARTRIDGES AND BALLISTICS

Once upon a time, if you purchased an AR-15, it came in one flavor, and that was .223 Remington. Similarly, the AR-10s were chambered in .308 Winchester. Today, cartridge options abound in both AR platforms. Some of these cartridges are commercial, SAAMI (Sporting Arms and Ammunition Institute) -approved cartridges, while others are proprietary or wildcat cartridges.

There are two primary reasons for the current multitude of cartridge options. First, as shooters began to appreciate the practicality of the AR, they also wanted to expand its applications. To do this, they sought out additional cartridges that would fit and function in the weapon. The other reason is that,

due to the modularity of both the AR-15 and AR-10, converting either to work with a new cartridge was as simple as installing a new and complete upper receiver or, in some cases, just a barrel.

It is not uncommon for an AR owner to have one lower receiver and multiple uppers, each upper in a different cartridge. Since the sighting system stays attached to the upper receiver, a shooter can switch between cartridges—receivers—and never have to readjust the sights or optics.

In the bolt-action or single-shot rifle world, switch-barrel rifles have always been desirable, but, in most cases, have been relegated to the custom market. This meant that they were not just expensive, they were also

There are more and more cartridges available for the AR-15 each year. Only time will tell which ones are to survive. Left to Right: .223 Remington, 6.8 SPC, 7.62x40 WT, .30 Remington AR, and .450 Bushmaster.

There are not many new cartridges being developed for the AR-10. This is mostly due to the fact that there has, for a long time, been a suitable batch of cartridges that work very well in this platform.

not all that easy to obtain. Often, someone desiring a switch-barrel rifle would be put on a waiting list, and then they would wait and wait.

With the AR, upper receivers are plentiful and easy to obtain. And, since they are not an item controlled by the ATF, they can be ordered by mail without the completion of any paperwork or background check. (An ATF Form 4473 is only required when transferring a complete AR or a lower receiver.) Again, the modularity of the AR has inherent value, and the ability to easily and quickly transition from one cartridge to another might be the ultimate expression of this versatility.

For the shooter who only wants one AR-15 or AR-10, the original chamberings—the .223 Remington or .308 Winchester, respectively—are probably the most practical options. But, for those who want to maximize the versatility of the firearm, either for hunting, sport shooting, self-defense, or even for law enforcement or military application, there are many options to choose from. To that point, here's a look at the most popular, commercially available AR-15 and AR-10 cartridges, their applications, and ballistics:

AR-15 CARTRIDGES

AR-15 cartridges are limited in overall length (OAL) by the AR-15 magazine, which will work with cartridges that have a maximum OAL of 2.26 inches or less. Another limiting factor is pressure. For a cartridge to be SAAMI-approved for an AR-15, it has to have a maximum average pressure (MAP) of no more than 55,000 psi.

.223 REMINGTON / 5.56 NATO

The .223 Remington came about during Armalite's development of the AR-15. Originally known as the .222 Special, it was a compromise cartridge, one with ballistic performance between the .222 Remington and the .222 Remington Magnum. The military's desire for even more velocity created the 5.56 NATO cartridge. That is the cartridge for which the military M16 rifle and M4 carbine are chambered. This has lead to much confusion and controversy, because the cartridge case dimensions for the .223 Remington and the 5.56 NATO are identical—well, almost.

If you measure and compare a .223 Remington case and a 5.56 NATO case by external dimensions alone, there is no difference. Where there is a difference is that, in most instances, the 5.56 NATO case has thicker walls, a design specification established by the military. Another difference is in MAP. The .223 Remington is held to a MAP of 55,000 psi by SAAMI, but the 5.56 NATO is *not* a SAAMI-approved cartridge and its MAP is about 5,000 psi higher. There's more. The chambers of the .223 Remington and the 5.56 NATO are actually cut differently. Not the part of the chamber that the

cartridge case fits in, but the section of the chamber immediately in front of the case known as the "lead" (pronounced "leed"). The lead in a 5.56 NATO chamber is longer than that of the "identical" .223 cartridge, and the bullets in 5.56 NATO ammo are loaded to work with this longer lead.

To put this in easy to understand terms, if you shoot a 5.56 NATO round in an AR-15 that has a .223 chamber, pressures can spike to more than 75,000 psi. What's that translate to? One round might work perfectly. Multiple rounds might impart stress that results in a broken gun or, worse, a broken gun and a broken shooter. On the other hand, it is perfectly safe to shoot .223 Remington ammunition in any AR-15 chambered for the 5.56 NATO. Many used to believe that this would result in poor accuracy, due to the longer lead in the 5.56 NATO chamber. Theoretically, that is a possibility, but, for the most part and in most cases, any degradation in accuracy is minimal.

With that lesson behind us, if you are purchasing an AR-15 and are having trouble deciding between one chambered for the 5.56 NATO or the .223 Remington, which one should you go with? Well, if you plan to shoot a lot of surplus military ammo, the choice is clear, go with the 5.56 NATO chambering. If, on the other hand, you only plan to shoot factory or handloaded .223

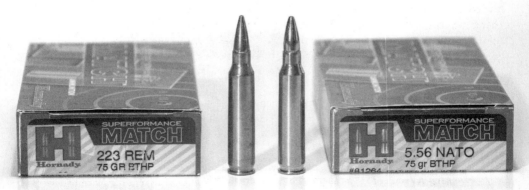

.223 Remington, left, next to a 5.56 NATO.

Remington ammo, there's no need to worry about the military version. That said, what you will want to consider next is the twist rate of the rifling.

Early on, the .223 Remington cartridge was most often loaded with 55-grain or lighter bullets. Very light bullets in a 1:14 twist rate will fly just fine, but that twist will not properly stabilize bullets heavier than 55 grains. So, you'll need to make a determination regarding what you want to do with your AR and what weight bullets you want to shoot through it. The chart to the right is a guide you can use to select twist rate, but, keep in mind that bullet *length*—not weight—is the determining factor; in some cases, lighter but very long bullets will need a faster twist rate.

Here's the thing about twist rate: err on the side of the faster twist. A 1: 9 twist will shoot a 55-grain bullet just fine and a 1:7 twist will shoot a 73-grain bullet just fine. It is very hard to over-stabilize a bullet and, at .223 Remington velocities, you don't have to worry about having them rip apart.

BULLET WEIGHT	TWIST RATE
55 grains or less	1:12
62-grain steel core M855 military ball	1 in 9
64- to 73-grain lead core bullets	1: 9
High ballistic coefficient (BC), VLD (Very Low Drag), long-range bullets	1: 8 or faster

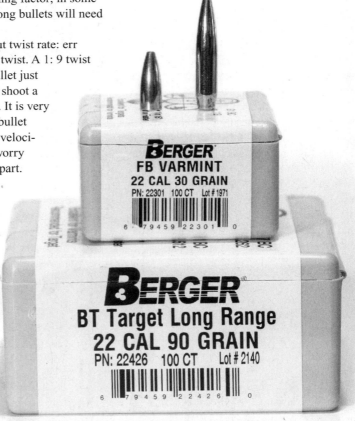

As you can see, there is a great deal of difference in length and weight, when it comes to the .22-caliber bullets that can be used in the .223 Remington. It's very important to match the rifling twist rate of your barrel to the type of bullet you will be shooting most often.

AR-15s in .223 are frequently used for shooting prairie dogs and gophers, as well as other vermin.

For best results on small varmints with the .223 Remington, choose explosive and lightweight varmint bullets.

Continuing the discussion of what you want to do with your AR, let's look at exactly what the .223 Remington cartridge is capable of. It is an excellent varmint—prairie dog, gopher, rock chuck and ground hog—cartridge out to around 500 yards. For larger varmints like coyotes, it will do the trick inside 400 yards. It can also be a very effective cartridge for deer-sized game out to around 250 yards.

The key to the proper application of the .223 Remington is in the choice of bullets. For the smallest varmints, select the lightweight, high-velocity bullets that will retain enough velocity to be explosive at long range. Hornady's 35-grain V-Max or Nosler's Ballistic Tips are good choices. For larger varmints like badgers and coyotes, about any expanding .223-caliber bullet will work, while for deer or wild hogs, you'll want to go with a deluxe big-game bullet like a Nosler Partition, Federal Fusion, Remington CoreLokt Ultra Bonded, or any of the Barnes Triple Shock bullets. These bullets expand wide, penetrate deep, and damage a lot of tissue. In fact, you can expect penetra-

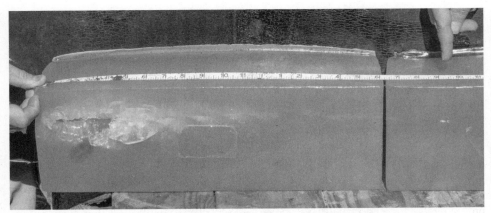

A good big-game bullet like the Barnes Triple Shock makes the .223 Remington perfectly suitable for deer-sized game. Terminal performance is similar to that of the .30-30 Winchester.

Many of the ammo companies now load Barnes Triple Shock bullets for the .223 Remington. Remington's new Hog Hammer line is a perfect example.

tion to be, in most cases, as good as what you'll see from a .30-30 Winchester.

To summarize the choice of an AR-15 in .223 Remington, what you will get is the most versatile of all the possible AR-15 chamberings. It is a cartridge that will work for the sport or competitive shooter, varmint or deer hunter, and even for personal protection. Its military and law enforcement suitability should be clear, as it is the standard service cartridge of the United States military and many police agencies. If you are going to have only one AR-15, it should probably be chambered for the 223 Remington /5.56 NATO.

.204 RUGER

The .204 Ruger was introduced, in 2004, as a joint venture between Hornady and Ruger. It was purposely designed as a varmint cartridge. From an AR-15 with a 20-inch barrel, the .204 Ruger can push a 32-grain bullet to 4,000 fps. It will not, however, hold up in the wind at longer ranges as well as the

.223 Remington, nor are there as many available factory ammunition options. However, if you intend to use your AR-15 for nothing but shooting small varmints, there's nothing wrong an AR in .204 Ruger.

.22 LR

The .22 Long Rifle (LR) is the world's most popular cartridge, and it has been around since 1887. It is affordable to shoot, relatively quiet, very accurate and, more than anything else, just plain fun. It also has a hunting application for small game and is, without question, the best first cartridge for new shooters.

Originally, .22 LR conversion kits, which used a different bolt carrier and a chamber insert, made it possible to shoot .22 LR ammo in AR-15s. The military was fond of these kits, but they were problematic and not very accurate. They did have training value. I remember, when working as the Training NCO for the National Guard CAV unit I was assigned to, we rigged an M16 with a .22

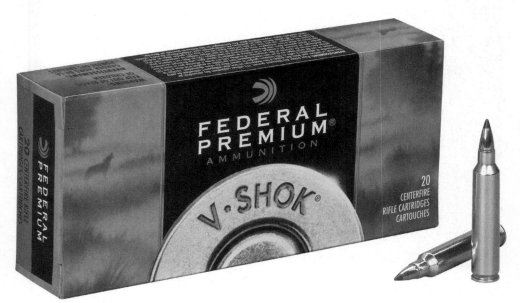

The .204 Ruger cartridge was purpose-built for shooting small varmints. It has become somewhat popular in the AR-15.

LR conversion kit to work coaxially with the main 105mm gun on an M 60 tank. This allowed us to conduct gunnery exercise while shooting at miniature tank targets at about 25 yards.

The next generation of .22 LR conversion kits for the AR-15 arrived in dedicated upper receivers. Extolling the virtues of the AR-15's modularity, a variety of companies offer a complete upper specifically for the .22 LR. In most cases, these upper receivers cost more than a comparable .22 semi-automatic rifle, but they do allow you to train, compete, hunt, and have fun with the same AR-15 lower you might use with a centerfire upper receiver.

More recently, we have seen a more affordable option, which is a .22 LR dedicated AR-15 built as a polymer lower and upper receiver. The Smith & Wesson M&P 15-22 is probably the best of the bunch and is comparatively priced to quality .22 LR

upper receivers. They are also reliable and accurate.

Don't expect your .22 LR upper receiver, or even a dedicated .22 LR AR-15, to operate with 100-percent reliability with low velocity or match .22 LR ammo. They are designed to work best with standard and, in some cases, high-velocity .22 LR loads. These are perfect for plinking, informal competition, sub-caliber training and, in a pinch, even for personal protection. In fact, my go-to home-defense weapon is a Smith & Wesson M&P 15-22 loaded with CCI Stinger ammunition. No, it's not the most powerful firearm in my home, but it is the only one everyone in my home— from my youngest daughter to my wife—can shoot accurately and with ease.

I find it hard to argue against owning either a .22 LR upper or a dedicated .22 LR AR-styled rifle, particularly if you already have an AR-15 in another cartridge, or even if you don't.

The .22 LR (left) is a great cartridge for the AR-15, because it allows high-volume, accurate, and affordable shooting.

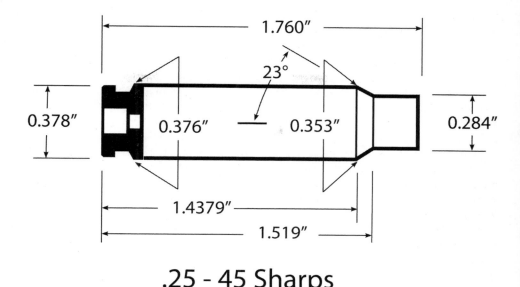

.25 - 45 Sharps

The .25-45 Sharps should be a great multi-purpose cartridge for the AR-15, but, at this writing, guns and ammo seem to be slow getting to market.

.25-45 SHARPS

Designed by the Sharps Rifle Company, this cartridge is nothing more than a .223 Remington case necked up to .257-caliber. It looks to be a great hunting cartridge for the AR-15, one almost duplicating the performance of the legendary .250 Savage cartridge with an 87-grain bullet. Though availability of ammo, upper receivers, and barrels is limited, this cartridge has great potential in the AR-15 platform.

6.5 GRENDEL

Developed by the company Alexander Arms, as a long-range cartridge that could take advantage of the very aerodynamic and high ballistic coefficient (BC) bullets in .264-caliber, the 6.5 Grendel has established an almost cult-like following. The cartridge is based on the Russian 7.62x39 cartridge and, when loaded with 120- to 130-grain bullets, works very well and reliably AR-15 magazines.

The 6.5 Grendel survived for many years as a proprietary cartridge, meaning brass and ammo were only available from Alexander Arms. However, in 2012, the cartridge was submitted to and approved by SAAMI. That opened up the manufacture of this ammunition to other companies. Only time will tell if the Grendel actually becomes mainstream. Currently, ammunition options are limited.

None of this takes away from the cartridge's performance. It can drive a 90-grain bullet to 3,000 feet per second (fps) and push a 120-grain bullet to almost 2,600 fps, which makes it one of the best long-range AR-15 cartridges overall, as well as a very fine hunting cartridge for varmints, hogs, and deer.

To convert an AR-15 in .223 Remington to 6.5 Grendel, you will need to rebuild your current upper receiver or opt for a new and complete upper receiver and magazines. A bonus: The 6.5 Grendel and the .264 LBC-AR cartridges are interchangeable.

6.8 REMINGTON SPC

Designed by Remington in conjunction with several members from the military, it was thought that the 6.8 SPC might replace the .223 Remington as the standard-issue service cartridge. This turned out not to be the case, but the 6.8 SPC has developed a good following from those who feel the .223 Remington isn't powerful enough for deer and hogs. From a 16-inch barreled AR-15, you can expect muzzle velocities with a 110-grain bullet to be about 2,500 fps.

The cartridge was based on the old .30 Remington, so its rim diameter is larger than that of the .223 Remington. This means a conversion will require a new and complete upper receiver or, at minimum, a new bolt, barrel, and magazines.

The future of the 6.8 SPC is questionable, due to the many new and larger-caliber AR-15 cartridges now becoming more available. However, it is a viable option and, next to the .223 Remington, there are probably more factory ammunition options for the 6.8 SPC than any other AR-15-compatible cartridge.

.300 AAC BLACKOUT

The concept of the .300 AAC Blackout was to provide both a subsonic and supersonic cartridge for the AR-15 that would launch a .30-caliber bullet, but still function with .223 Remington/5.56 NATO magazines. The cartridge was developed and submitted to SAAMI by Advanced Armament Corporation (AAC), which worked on the cartridge in con-

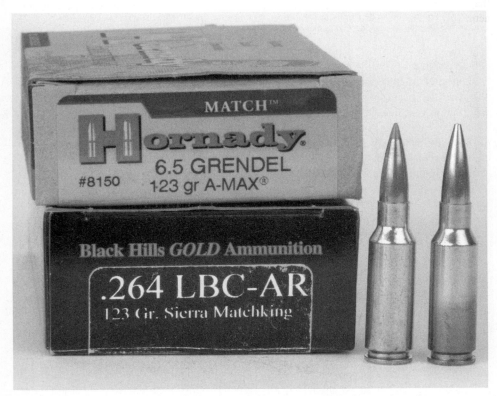

The 6.5 Grendel is probably the most successful of the wildcat cartridges designed for the AR-15, but without using the .223 Remington cartridge case.

junction with Remington. It is nothing more than a legitimized version of the .300 Whisper wildcat cartridge developed by J.D. Jones.

In its supersonic form, the .300 AAC Blackout offers external and terminal ballistics similar to what you would expect from a .30-30 Winchester cartridge when loaded with 125-grain bullets. With subsonic ammo and a suppressor, the Blackout has minimal recoil and generates minimal audible and visual signatures.

Part of the marketing hype behind this cartridge is that it offers one answer to both supersonic and subsonic fire. That's only partly true. If you want your AR in .300 Blackout to shoot both subsonic and supersonic ammo with 100-percent reliability, you will need to opt for an upper receiver that has an adjustable gas block. Still, does it actually serve both purposes?

After a good deal of testing factory supersonic and subsonic ammunition for the Blackout on paper and shooting it into 10-percent gelatin, it is my opinion that what this cartridge really offers is a great launching pad for the subsonic ammo. If a supersonic .30-caliber bullet is what you want, the 7.62x40 WT and the .30 Remington AR are both more powerful options. In other words, the .300 AAC Blackout is not the perfect answer to *both* subsonic and supersonic applications. It has, however, become a very popular cartridge, if for no other reason than it has a cool name. Supersonic loads are available for about any application you might demand of it, and a variety of subsonic loads can be found, too. There are even some subsonic loads from Lehigh Defense that will expand at subsonic velocities.

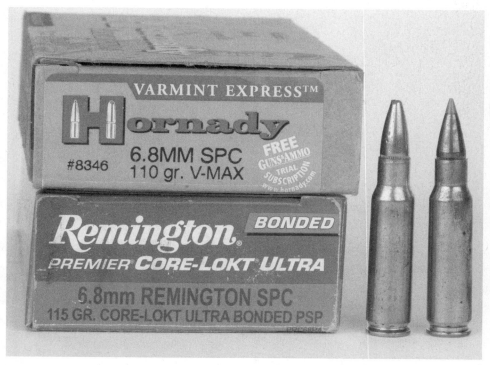

The 6.8 SPC Remington cartridge is measurably more powerful than the .223 Remington. However, hunters using both for deer and hogs will probably not be able to notice any measurable difference in performance.

7.62X40 WT

This cartridge was developed by Bill Wilson, of Wilson Combat, as an option to both the .300 AAC Blackout and the .30 Remington AR. Wilson is an avid hog hunter, averaging almost a hog per day on his ranch in Texas. He had become very fond of the .30 Remington AR, but, due to the fact that he hunts most often at night, and the fact that Remington wasn't offering brass for the .30 Rem AR, Wilson got tired of looking around in the high grass and rattlesnakes for empty cases.

Wilson had experimented with the .300 AAC Blackout, and while he was convinced it was a great subsonic cartridge for the AR, he wanted more performance—velocity—for supersonic loads. His solution was simple: Cut the .223 Remington case back to 40mm and neck it up to .30-caliber. There's plenty of .223 brass out there, and the additional case capacity over the .300 AAC would give him about an additional 200 fps.

Having a good bit of experience with this cartridge I can attest to its accuracy and effectiveness on hogs. My son and I killed a dozen or more medium-sized feral hogs while hunting with Bill, in Texas. Currently, Wilson Combat is the only manufacturer offering loaded ammunition or brass, but Wilson hopes this will change and that other manufacturers will recognize the versatility of this supersonic cartridge for hunting, competition, and tactical applications.

Wilson's extensive testing has shown that .30-caliber bullets weighing between 110 and 125 grains are best stabilized with a 1:12 twist. This suggested slower twist rate and slightly higher case capacity are the main

Several supersonic loads for the .300 AAC Blackout are available and all can be expected to deliver good terminal performance for deer and similarly sized game.

differences between the .300 AAC Blackout and the 7.62x40 WT, the latter of which is intended only as a supersonic cartridge. A new barrel is all that's needed to go from an AR in .223 Remington to one in 7.62x40 WT; .223 magazines will work just fine.

.30 REMINGTON AR

This cartridge has been one of the most important cartridge introductions since the .223 Remington. It was the first and has been the only cartridge capable of truly moving the AR-15 platform into the big-game mar-

There is no shortage of subsonic factory ammunition for the .300 AAC Blackout. While many of the loads utilize the same, heavy-for-caliber bullet, Lehigh Defense is the only company offering a .30-caliber load that will expand at subsonic velocities.

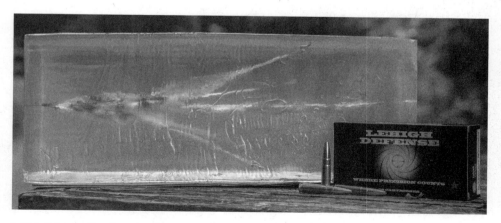

Lehigh Defense offers the only subsonic expanding bullet for the .300 Blackout. It is a better option for personal protection and hunting than the non-expanding subsonic loads.

ket. The problem was, Remington screwed up its introduction by not having rifles, ammo, and brass available. Additionally, Remington also published bad ballistic information on the cartridge that made it look no better than the 7.62x39 Russian cartridge. Compounding all these mistakes was the fact that it was introduced during a time when politics were driving the purchase of ARs to the point of a frenzy; the buying public wanted the AR they thought they might not be able to get, which was a carbine-length rifle in .223 Remington. The *last* thing they were thinking about was a new AR rifle for

hunting, and hunting applications are where the .30 Remington AR shines.

A man by the name of Randy Grove, working at Remington, designed this cartridge. He started with a .450 Bushmaster case, but increased the rim diameter from 0.473 to 0.492. This meant the cartridge case could not be formed from existing brass. The end result was a .30-caliber cartridge that can push a 125-grain bullet to 2,800 fps, and a 150-grain bullet to 2,600 fps, from a 22-inch barreled AR-15.

From an external and terminal performance standpoint, no other AR-15 cartridge

The Wilson Combat 7.62x40 WT cartridge is a great .30-caliber option for the AR, particularly if you want to keep the high magazine capacity for which the platform is known. Wilson Combat offers a variety of loads.

This 200-pound wild boar was taken with a single shot from an AR chambered for the 7.62x40 WT cartridge.

The .30 Remington AR has proven it can deliver very good terminal performance with both factory rounds and handloads. It has the power and range for hunting any game in North America.

Critters as large and tough as black bears are no match for the .30 Remington AR, which is the most powerful cartridge commercially available in the AR-15 platform.

comes close. I jumped on board the .30 Remington AR bus immediately and hunted with and handloaded for it extensively. It is incredibly accurate and sufficient for taking game as large as elk, as long as ranges are kept to within 300 yards.

Currently, Remington is the only manufacturer offering ammo and, at this writing, it offers five loads. Brass for handloaders has now become available, but, with the intense increase in AR ownership over the last five years, I feel the only real hope for the .30 Remington AR is for Remington to begin offering .30 Remington uppers which, in conjunction with a different magazine, is what's needed to convert an AR in .223 Remington to .30 Remington AR. Nevertheless, if you want to hunt big game with an AR-15 or AR-10, your search for a cartridge can start and end with this cartridge.

7.62X39 RUSSIAN

Designed by the Soviets during WWII for the RPD machine gun, this cartridge gained its fame in the AK-47. Even though it has the same 7.62 designation as the .308 Winchester, which is a .308-caliber cartridge, the 7.62x39 utilizes a 0.312-caliber bullet; modern ammunition and rifle bore diameters can vary between .308 and .312 diameter. With regards to the cartridge's suitability in an AR-15, the excessive taper on the case has been notorious for causing feeding problems. This is why magazines for the AK-47 are curved like a banana. Ballistically, the 7.62x39 is very close to the .300 AAC Blackout, but, unlike that round, you can purchase 7.62x39 ammo from many manufacturers. On the flip side, of all the ammo available for this cartridge, there's not actually a large selection of loads suitable for hunting.

9MM LUGER

Though only really popular in law enforcement circles, AR-15s chambered for the 9mm Luger pistol cartridge are available. Their application beyond fun and personal protection is limited. Given that an AR-15 in 9mm

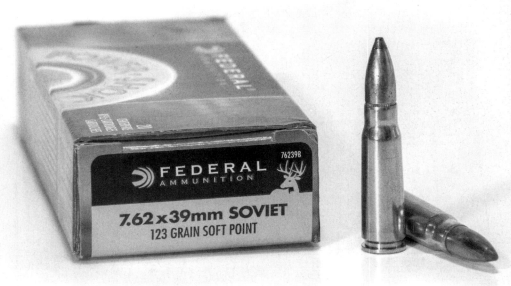

The 7.62x39 Soviet has seen limited success in the AR platform. Today, there are numerous, better-performing .30-caliber cartridges that will work in the AR-15.

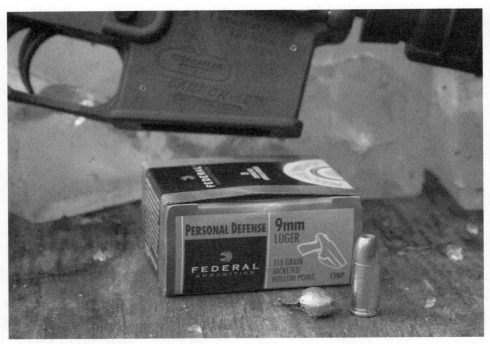

A 9mm bullet fired from a short-barreled rifle like an AR-15 can create a nasty and deadly wound, but it's no more effective at stopping a threat than the .223 Remington.

The .450 Bushmaster is one of the largest-caliber cartridges to ever be designed for the AR-15 platform. It hits hard on both ends, but range is limited.

is no smaller than one in .223, the attraction to this configuration is, for the most part, one of shooting affordability and a lack of recoil. However some law enforcement agencies do use 9mm ARs in subsonic configurations.

.450 BUSHMASTER

Originally based on the rebated rim .284 Winchester case, the .450 Bushmaster is a straight-wall case that is very similar, ballistically, to the old .45-70 Government cartridge. Initially, it looked like the .450 Bushmaster was going to be a raging success, but interest soon dwindled, likely because of the lack of a wide enough range of suitable factory loads for hunting—and hunting was about the one and only use for the cartridge due to its rainbow-like trajectory and heavy recoil.

AR-15s in .450 Bushmaster seemed to be a bit finicky, and some had incurable feeding issues. Hornady and Remington are currently the only two manufacturers loading ammunition for this cartridge. While it does push a big heavy bullet, from a terminal performance standpoint, it offers no real advantage over the flatter shooting .30 Remington AR.

AR-10 CARTRIDGES

Unlike the ever growing number of AR-15 cartridges, which exhibit a wide range of rim diameters and cartridge dimensions, for the most part, all the cartridges commonly chambered in the AR-10 are based on its original cartridge chambering, the .308 Winchester/7.62 NATO. And, as it is with the AR-15, the AR-10's original cartridge is the one that remains the most popular and, for all intents and purposes, the most practical. Still, options exist.

.243 WINCHESTER

Since 1955, the .243 has been one of the most versatile sporting cartridges ever created. It is equally effective at shooting groundhogs, coyotes, and deer, and that versatility has been its appeal—one cartridge that will do most of what many hunters want to do. Most every manufacturer offers ammo for the .243 and in a wide array of bullet weights and styles.

I have a decent amount of time in the field hunting, as well as on the bench, with the .243 Winchester firing out of the AR-10 platform. It is really quite gentle on the shoulder and, with bullets weights ranging from 55 to 100 grains, it offers solutions for a wide range of pursuits. Though it could be employed for sport shooting or as a tactical arm, the AR-10 in the .243 is best suited to hunting.

The .243 Winchester is one of the most versatile hunting cartridges for varmints and medium-sized big game. It will even work for game as large as elk.

This fine South Texas whitetail was taken with a Remington Model R25 in .243 Winchester using a 95-grain Accutip bullet. The range to the buck was 200 yards.

The 6.5 Creedmoor continues to gain popularity as an AR cartridge.

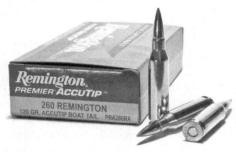

The .260 Remington will make a great big-game cartridge for anyone wanting to hunt with an AR-10.

6.5 CREEDMOOR

Though only offered in a few factory AR-10 rifles, the 6.5 Creedmoor does have application in this platform, specifically if shooting at long range is on the menu. It uses highly aerodynamic 6.5-caliber bullets and was purpose-built for those bullets, which is the main reason the case shape of the 6.5 Creedmoor differs from that of the .260 Remington.

.260 REMINGTON

Like the .243 Winchester, the .260 Remington is nothing more than a .308 Winchester necked down to a smaller caliber. In the .260's case, this caliber is 6.5 (just like the 6.5 Grendel, with a bullet diameter of .264). Cartridges of this caliber have never really caught on in America, and the same can be said for the .260. This has never

made much sense; 6.5-caliber bullets are often very aerodynamic, due to their high ballistic coefficient. If you want to stretch the range of your AR-10 while hunting deer or while on the range, the .260 Remington is an excellent choice. Most manufacturers offer ammo for the .260, and while selection is not extensive, there are more .260 Remington ammo options than there are 6.5 Creedmoor.

7MM-08 REMINGTON

As it is with the 6.5 Creedmoor and the .260 Remington, in the AR-10, the 7mm-08 isn't all that popular a chambering. For all practical purposes, it offers ballistics right in the middle of what you would expect from a .260 Remington and a .308 Winchester. On the plus side, there is a good selection of factory loads available.

The 7mm-08 is not a very popular chambering in the AR-10. This is mostly because anything the 7mm-08 (left) can do, so can the .308 Winchester.

When it comes to cartridges for the AR-10, it's hard to argue against the .308 Winchester, unless you intend to hunt smaller game. It is accurate, offers plenty of power, and factory ammunition options abound.

.308 WINCHESTER

There's no question that the .308 Winchester is one of the most popular cartridges of all time. Its use by the military in machine guns and sniper rifles and its suitability for almost every big-game species on the planet has ensured its success. It is a true 400-yard deer cartridge, and you will find more suitable big-game loads for this cartridge, from more manufacturers, than any other. It's hard to go wrong with a .308, regardless the type of rifle you choose.

The .308 Winchester was introduced in 1952 and is identical to the 7.62 NATO cartridge. Due to the wide selection of factory ammo available, in bullet weights from as light as 110 grains to as heavy as 180 grains, twist rate can become an issue. A twist rate of 1:10 is the most popular for AR-10s and is the correct choice. It will allow you to accurately shoot the light bullets, as well as the long and heavy options.

.338 FEDERAL

The .338 Federal is one of the newest chamberings to become available in the AR-10, and it is also the one of the newest cartridges based on the .308 Winchester case. Even though, in a very short time, it has become a trusted big-game cartridge, ballistically there's not much difference between the .308 Winchester and the .338 Federal. In truth, the only reason to opt for the larger-caliber .338 Federal—which is nothing more than a .308 necked up to .338—would be if you wanted to also hunt game larger than deer and liked the idea of a heavier bullet. On the downside, ammo availability is limited, as are lighter bullet weights in factory ammo.

The .338 Federal is nothing more than the .308 Winchester cartridge necked up to .338-caliber.

AR 15 & AR 10 CARTRIDGE COMPARISONS

AR 15 CARTRIDGES	BW	MV/ME	V 100	V/T 200	V/T 300	V/T 400
.204 Ruger	32 gr.	3500/870	3029	2603/-1	2219/-7	1867/-20
.204 Ruger	45 gr.	3200/1023	2820	2471/-1	2144/-9	1850/-24
.223 Remington	40 gr.	3700/1215	3190	2808/-1	2147/-9	1850/-16
.223 Remington	55 gr.	3240/1281	2885	2558/-1	2254/-8	1970/-21
.223 Remington	60 gr.	3160/1330	2755	2384/-1	2094/-10	1734/-26
.223 Remington	69 gr.	2850/1276	2650	2372/-2	2151/-11	1942/-27
.223 Remington	45 gr.	3550/1259	2978	2475/-1	2024/-8	1627/-2
6.5 Grendel	123 gr.	2580/1818	2410	2247/-3	2090/-14	1940/-32
6.8 Remington SPC	115 gr.	2625/1759	2345	2083/-3	1838/-15	1614/-37
.300 Blackout	110 gr.	2480/1465	2300	1921/-4	1686/-18	1474/-43
.300 Blackout	125 gr.	2250/1442	2042	1846/-5	1663/-21	1495/-50
.300 Blackout	220 gr.	1000/488	969	942/-34	917/-107	894/-222
7.62 X 40 WT	110 gr.	2540/1575	2261	1999/-4	1757/-17	1538/-41
.30 Remington AR	125 gr.	2800/2175	2564	2340/-2	2128/-11	1927/-28
.30 Remington AR	150 gr.	2550/2165	2361	2181/-3	2008/-14	1844/-33
9mm Luger	115 gr.	1375/482	1120	903/-13	804/-31	724/-224
.450 Bushmaster	250 gr.	2200/2686	1840	1524/-8	1268/-32	N/A
AR 10 CARTRIDGES	**BW**	**MV/ME**		**V/T 200**	**V/T 300**	**V/T 400**
.243 Winchester	55 gr.	3750/1717	3365	3013/-1	2688/-4	2386/-13
.243 Winchester	85 gr.	3260/2005	2923	2615/-1	2350/-7	2101/-20
.243 Winchester	100 gr.	2800/1740	2575	2361/-2	2157/-11	1963/-27
6.5 Creedmoor	129 gr.	2950/2493	2190	2571/-2	2393/-8	2222/-21
.260 Remington	120 gr.	2800/2088	2590	2445/-2	2278/-10	2117-25
.260 Remington	140 gr.	2700/2265	2500	2336/-2	2165/-12	2001/-28
7mm-08 Remington	140 gr.	2790/2419	2571	2362/-2	2163/-11	1974/-27
.308 Winchester	150 gr.	2800/2610	2589	2388/-2	2196/-11	2013/-26
.308 Winchester	165 gr.	2650/2572	2467	2291/-2	2123/-12	1962/-29
.308 Winchester	175 gr.	2570/2566	2403	2243/-3	2089/-13	1941/-31
.308 Winchester	180 gr.	2600/2701	2449	2303/-3	2162/-12	2026/-29
.338 Federal	180 gr.	2800/3133	2568	2347/-2	2138/-11	1939/-28

Note: This chart lists the muzzle velocity and muzzle energy for a selection of factory-produced AR-15 and AR-10 compatible cartridges. The results are more nominal than precise, but give a reasonable picture of the ballistic capabilities of each cartridge. The trajectory reflects a 100-yard zero and a scope height of 2.75 inches, which is common to the AR platform. The remaining velocity and drop below line of sight is shown at 200, 300, and 400 yards. Downrange kinetic energy is computable with the following formula: Energy = (v2 x b)/450,400 where v = velocity in fps and b = bullet weight in grains.

CHAPTER 6

OPEN SIGHTS

The original AR was revolutionary in its design for several reasons, and the way the sights were integrated into the weapon platform was one of them. As revolutionary as this design was, because the sights were fitted to the rifle's carry handle, they would prove to be the only major and almost mandated modification to the modern AR, whether the customer is a soldier, police officer, or civilian.

On the original M16/AR-15, the rear sight was integral to the carry handle, which was also integral to the upper receiver. This provided a rugged housing for the rear sight, and it also positioned the sight at the correct height for a shooter to comfortably look through, while maintaining a cheek weld on a stock that was straight in line with—and not below—the barrel.

The problem with this concept was that as cool as the carry handle seemed to be, other than elevating the sight the proper amount above the barrel, it served no other purpose. The only time any solider (or anyone else) ever used the carry handle to carry the weapon was when they were in some sort of administrative setting or if they were wounded and trying to get their ass off the battlefield or to cover.

There was another problem, too. If the carry handle became damaged in some way, then the sights were damaged too; this also meant the upper receiver had to be replaced completely. As you can imagine, that's an expensive operation, one that takes half the weapon out of service, and that kind of damage was something that could easily occur. A

On the original M16/AR-15, the rear sight was integral to the carry handle, a feature now rare on modern ARs.

bullet could hit the handguard, a tank could run over it, or it could get bent by any other number of circumstances on the battlefield.

The front sight was really no different. It was integral to the gas block on original ARs and was fixed in place at the proper height to match with the rear sight/carry handle. Here again you had an issue: If the sight became damaged, it required maintenance and repair that was above the operator level. In other words, the weapon had to be removed from service to correct a broken sight. Not good.

Original ARs came with a fixed front sight that was integral to the gas block. For the most part, modern ARs no longer have this style front sight.

This AR is equipped with a prismatic optical sight, a fixed front sight, and a folding rear sight. If the shooter so desires, he could raise the rear sight, and it will co-witness through the optical sight.

This AR has a flat-top upper receiver with a detachable rear sight, but it retains the fixed front sight. It provides a much more optics-friendly platform than did the original design.

The other intrinsic problem with this sighting system was that it wasn't conducive to the mounting of optics. Yes, it is true that optics mounts were configured to work with the carry handle, but this placed the line of sight for the shooter well above the stock, making it impossible to obtain a cheek weld. Additionally, a single screw attached the optics to these carry handle mounts, and a single screw is never a good idea when you're mounting optics.

Initially, after the flat-top upper receiver became popular, the fixed front sight was retained. This worked reasonably well; a shooter could install a rear sight that attached to the flat-top Picatinny rail. However, if a low-power optic was attached to the flat-top receiver, then the fixed front sight was visible through the optic. This could be a good or bad thing, depending on how you looked at it (pun intended). You see, even at the turn of the century, many shooters, especially military personnel, were still not all that trusting of an optical sight's ability to survive the harsh conditions of combat or the battlefield. Indeed, many considered it a good idea to have a fold-down rear sight mounted in tandem with the optical sight and a fixed front

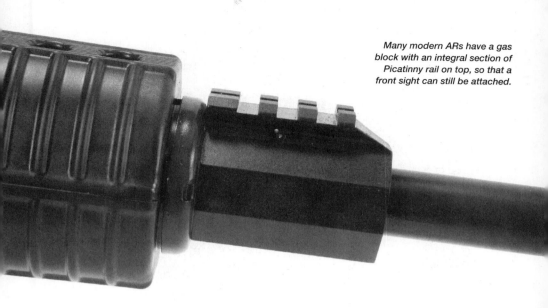

Many modern ARs have a gas block with an integral section of Picatinny rail on top, so that a front sight can still be attached.

sight. If attention to the mounting height of the optic was paid, the shooter could use the optic or he could flip up the rear sight and aim with the sights by looking through the optic. This sight configuration is known as "co-witnessing" and, in tactical circles, it is still common practice and thought by many to be the only way to configure a tactical AR-style carbine's sight system.

Competition shooters and hunters did not like the fixed front sight, so, as the AR platform gained acceptance across a wider audience of shooters, gas blocks without a front sight became more common. Some were made with a short section of Picatinny rail on the top, so that a removable front sight could be attached if desired. Those using the AR in competition found they were being required more and more frequently to engage targets that were near and far over the same course of fire, and, so, such sighting arrangements found great application.

Since the sights on an AR are high above the bore, this means that, when you are

Due to the nature of the design, sights for an AR must be mounted high above the bore, so that the shooter can get their eye behind them.

Though this AR does not have sights, it does have an optic and a reflex sight mounted above the optic. The reflex sight is zeroed for close targets and the optic for long-range targets.

Whether it's on an AR that's a dedicated .22 LR or the more common AR in .223 Remington, the most common configuration is a flat-top upper receiver and a free-floating handguard with a top rail.

Since the rear sight of the AR is close to the shooter's eye, the aperture sight system is the most logical choice.

shooting at very close range, as close as just several feet, your sights will be pointing to a spot about two inches above where the bullet will strike. This may or may not be an issue, depending on your target. The obvious answer, of course, is to hold high, but the problems with holding high are that it is a guess and that it is also something you may not remember to do under stress.

With the advent of the Picatinny rail, tools, attachments, and accessories soon became available that gave AR shooters options, when it came time to engage close targets. Compact reflex sights were mounted in tandem with a primary optic that was zeroed for shooting at longer distances, the compact reflex sight subsequently zeroed at a very close range. Sometimes these redundant sight configurations were also used in conjunction with open sights, providing three sights system for one rile. All could be effectively zeroed at different distances, just as they could all be zeroed at the same range.

It should be obvious that no other long-gun offers this type of versatility, which, for the most part, came about due to the poor design or inefficiency of the original sighting system. As it is with every other aspects of the AR, the options when it comes to sights are just as endless, and the way these sights can be configured together or sepa-

These flip-up sights from Magpul are called MBUS (Magpul Back-Up Sights) sights and are an affordable and reliable sight system for an AR. They work great in conjunction with optics, because they can be folded down and out of the way.

rately only enhances the immense versatility of the AR system.

Without question, the most common configuration of an AR today is one with a flat-top upper receiver and a free-floating handguard that either has an integral top rail or will permit the installation of one. Manufactures have learned that most who purchase an AR like to arrange their AR to suit them, so it is also very common for new ARs to come without open sights at all. There's no reason to sell a customer something they're only going to take off, just as there's no reason to purchase an AR with sights you do not intend to use.

Through all this, the open sighting configuration for the AR has remained an aperture rear sight and a post front sight. There is a reason that the traditional blade-type rear sight which is common on traditional bolt, lever, pump and other rifles wasn't used and that is because the rear sight needs to be very close to the shooter's eye on an AR. If a bladed sight were placed that close to the eye, it would simply be too out of focus to work. The aperture sight

circumvents this focusing problem, because your eye does not have to focus on it. It can remain slightly fuzzy and your eye will naturally, with a bit of practice, center the front post within that hazy circle.

Another reason for the close proximity of the rear sight to the eye was to increase the sight radius—the distance between the front and rear sight. You see, the greater this distance, the less deviations in sight picture will affect the disparity between the point of aim (POA) and point of impact (POI). As an analogy, consider a handgun. Handguns are generally harder to shoot accurately at any distance, because of their short sight radiuses.

Most modern ARs have 16-inch barrels, and this means that the sight radius is also only about 16 inches, even with the aperture sight mounted at the rear of the upper receiver. If a traditional blade-type sight were to be mounted on the barrel at about the same place as you'd find one mounted on a lever-action rifle, the resulting sight radius would be only about half that—and, with that type of sight arrangement, shooting an

Many AR rear sights come with two apertures that can be utilized simply by flipping the aperture 90 degrees. The small hole is better for precision shooting at longer ranges.

By flipping the aperture on the rear sight, you have access to a larger hole or peep. This is generally considered better when shooting at close range or in dynamic situations.

AR would be similar to shooting a long-barreled handgun.

Original and early AR aperture sights had two apertures. One had a small hole for shooting at long range, the other a large hole for shooting up close. These apertures were commonly offset, too, which meant that, if you switched between the apertures (by flipping the aperture), your point of impact would be different. This is something you need to be aware of with both older aperture sights and newer designs.

The original sight system, which was incorporated into the handguard, was adjustable. You moved the rear sight to correct for windage (horizontal error), and you moved the front sight to correct for trajectory (vertical error). The next incarnation of sights for the AR are generally referred to as A2-style sights. This carry handle sight allowed the rear sight to be adjusted for both windage and elevation. This was a definite improvement, since adjustments of the A1 or original style sight were rugged, but cumbersome.

Modern AR sights, which are designed to attach to a flat-top upper receiver, can be had in numerous configurations. Some will allow full adjustment of the front and rear sight, while some are more traditional in design, where the rear sight can be adjusted for windage and the front sight for elevation. However, manufacturers have become much more clever in how these adjustments are made, and adjusting modern sights is much easier than adjusting the sights on the original AR-15/M16.

The other trend dominating the AR sight market is the fold-down/flip-up sight. These sights can be folded out of the way so that they do not interfere with either a traditional rifle scope or even a more modern reflex, holographic, or prismatic sight. These sights can also be adjusted so that when they are flipped up, they can co-witness through an optic, providing either the same or a different zero. Several companies also offer redundant open sights for use when an optic fails or for when the target is very close. Many 3-Gun competitors utilize this type of sight, for

Many modern AR rear sights offer both windage and elevation adjustment. This is handy, but not necessary.

engaging targets at breath-smelling distances. Some of these sights are mounted at a 45-degree angle to the flat-top upper receiver and, to use them, all the shooter needs to do is rotate the AR about 40 degrees to the left and look down the sights. As unwieldy as this may sound, it is relatively easy and comfortable to accomplish.

The different types and styles of AR open sights is simply too vast to cover with any detail here. What needs to happen is that you must decide, depending on how you intend to employ your AR, which sights are best for you. This may take some experimenting and you may even find that, depending on what you want, more than one option is ideal. You may also find that you like the idea of redundant, co-witnessed sight systems or no open sights at all on your AR. The beautiful part is that a change is only a turn of a few screws away.

Designed more like pistol sights, these sights from XS Sights mount at an angle and provide an ultra-close range sight or a back-up sight to an optic in case it fails.

CHAPTER 7

OPTICAL SIGHTS

The Trijicon 1-6x VCOG is an example of one of the most advanced optical sights ever designed for an AR. It incorporates an illuminated ballistic reticle and an integral mounting system.

The days of the AR with the fixed carry handle and open sights are almost gone. The advent of the flat-top upper receiver changed all that. With it, shooters could mount any type of optical sight they wanted or opt for a detachable carry handle with open sights. The flat-top upper receiver revolutionized the AR and increased its versatility exponentially.

Your optical sighting options for the AR are endless. In short, you can utilize any rifle scope you might otherwise mount on any traditional rifle, or you can go with some sort of red dot sight. We'll look at all of these, but, before you even attempt to sort through the pile of optical options, you need to take a serious look at how you intend to employ your AR. You should also consider whether or not you will be using multiple upper receivers on the same lower, so that you can use your AR for multiple things. This might necessitate several different optical sights, one for each upper and depending on what you want to do with each.

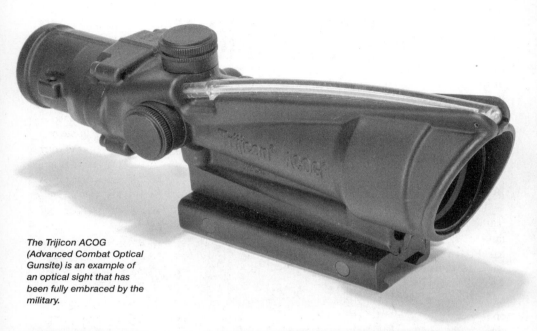

The Trijicon ACOG (Advanced Combat Optical Gunsite) is an example of an optical sight that has been fully embraced by the military.

With the railed, flat-top upper receiver, you can switch back and forth between optical sights as your needs dictate.

Let's look at the variety of ways in which you can effectively employ an AR. This will give you a better understanding of your optical needs. The best way to do this is to establish categories such as tactical, hunting, sport, and recreation. Within each of these categories would also exist subcategories or specialized applications. This is where the glass meets the gun, you might say, and choosing an optical sight based on the subcategory you intend to participate in the most will provide the best optical accompaniment to your AR.

TACTICAL

The AR platform was conceived to be a battle rifle, and that is where it has won its fame. History has shown that the military has driven civilian trends in firearms, but, with optical sights, the reverse is true. Only during our latest conflict in the Middle East have optical sights become commonplace on individual infantry weapons. The optical sights most used on the AR by the military would tend to fall into the red dot sight category. However, all optical sights that are called red dot sights are not really red dot sights at all. More on that shortly.

PERSONAL PROTECTION/CLOSE COMBAT

The AR is becoming more and more popular as a personal-defense firearm. When I say "personal-defense," I don't mean one carried on a day-to-day basis, but rather one that is kept in the home or at a business for protection from everyday vagabonds and bad guys, to a gun that is kept ready in the case of a natural disaster where looting and lawlessness might occur. In these types of situations, it could be reasonably assumed that engagement distances would be relatively close and shots may need to be taken at a moment's notice. Red dot-style sights tend to shine in these kinds of situations, and those built for the military have proven to be very rugged under what you can imagine are some pretty tough conditions.

Meopta's M-RAD is a highly advanced red dot sight suitable for up-close engagements.

By combing an EOTech holographic sight with a magnifier that can be flipped to the side, you double the versatility of a non-magnifying sight.

For really close-in shooting, say, inside 50 yards, magnification is more of a hindrance than it is a help. Instead, it's optical sights that allow the shooter to keep both eyes open that tend to get the nod, and that is exactly why S.W.A.T. operators commonly use these kinds of sights.

GENERAL UTILITY

An AR that might be used for both personal protection and survival could be tasked with both up-close shots and shots at extended ranges. If you are trying to engage an aggressor at 300 yards with an optical sight that provides no magnification, it's doable, but not ideal. For this reason, optical devices known as "magnifiers" have become popular. They can be mounted between the shooter's eye and the zero-magnification red dot style sight. A magnifier will generally magnify the image by three times and, if installed correctly, it can be flipped out of the way to allow for the use of the red dot-style sight if the distance to the target shortens.

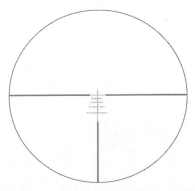

Long-range tactical optics typically have a Mil Dot or ballistic reticle to aid in trajectory compensation at long range.

PRECISION/LONG RANGE

From a civilian standpoint, the tactical application of an AR in a long-range scenario might be difficult to justify. Also as a civilian, it's hard to come up with a situation where you *should* be shooting at attackers at distances beyond 300 yards.

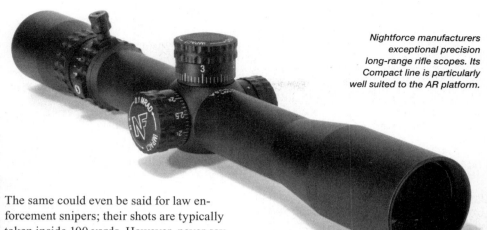

Nightforce manufacturers exceptional precision long-range rifle scopes. Its Compact line is particularly well suited to the AR platform.

The same could even be said for law enforcement snipers; their shots are typically taken inside 100 yards. However, never say never. If you want or believe you need an AR equipped for precision or long-range shooting, you will need an appropriate optic. Ideally, this would be a traditionally styled rifle scope with target turrets and a graduated MIL, MOA, or ballistic reticle. The extent of magnification required will be the question, and the standard answer is you will need at least 1x of magnification for every 100 yards you intend to shoot. A variable scope is the best option, because it will also allow you to dial down the magnification if the engagement distances get close, therefore not sacrificing the close-range capabilities of the firearm.

HUNTING

About the only things you cannot hunt successfully with an AR would be the big, dangerous game species in Africa, and that's mostly because you cannot take an AR to Africa to hunt with. Here in the United States, where you can hunt with an AR of some sort in any state but Pennsylvania, all the game animals are on the table. Still, as a hunter, you should realize that different pursuits are best served with optical sights that offer certain advantages.

For most hunting situations a common 3-9x rifle scope will work perfectly well on any AR.

High-magnification rifle scopes like this Leupold VX2 with a 6-18x magnification range and an adjustable objective are great for high-volume varmint hunting, when small targets are involved.

GENERAL HUNTING

For general hunting, the standard, variable-style scope with a magnification range of between 2-7x or 3-9x is about ideal. There are still lots of decisions to be made beyond this, such as do you want an illuminated reticle and/or a ballistic reticle? Should you get a scope with a large objective so that it is brighter? Do you need a one-inch or 30mm tube? The answer to most of these questions is personal preference, but do keep in mind that the larger the objective on the scope, the higher it will need to be mounted, and this can impact your cheek weld and how the AR will fit you.

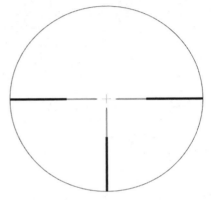

For predator calling, consider a traditional rifle scope with an illuminated reticle.

HIGH-VOLUME VARMINT HUNTING

High-volume varmint hunting is typically done from a portable shooting bench that is carried into a prairie dog or gopher town. Hunters will set up on these benches and, in some cases, shoot all day from one location. High-magnification scopes are generally the rule for this pursuit, and a variable scope with a range of 4-14x would seem ideal. Target turrets, ballistic reticles, and an adjustable parallax are well suited to this type of shooting, too.

PREDATOR CALLING

A general-purpose rifle scope will work well here, but there are some additional considerations. Sometimes predator calling is conducted in low light and even in the dark, so an illuminated reticle isn't a bad idea. By the same token, a rifle scope that performs

well in low light situations is a good idea, while the use of night vision devices that work in conjunction with a rifle scope is becoming popular where legal. If this latter is the route you want to go, you should consider the compatibility of the scope with these kinds of optical device.

BIG-GAME HUNTING

A big-game scope for an AR could be just about anything, but to best match the scope to your hunt, consider the terrain over which you will be hunting and the type of shooting situation with which you will most likely be presented. The old standby 3-9x40mm scope is always a solid choice, but, as it is with predator hunting, illuminated reticles and low light performance are valid considerations. So would be ballistic

Trijicon's Accupoint rifle scopes all have illuminated reticles, regardless the reticle design. They are a great choice for big-game hunting.

reticles and target turrets in situations where long shots might be the rule.

HOG ERADICATION

The AR has become a very popular firearm for hog hunting and hog eradication, for several reasons. The AR will allow for a fast follow-up shot, and it is compatible with a variety of optical sights. If you are hunting hogs over a feeder at about 100 yards, about any optical sight will do. If you are hunting them at night, night vision-compatible optics or, at a minimum, an illuminated reticle, are a must. Shooting feral hogs from a chopper is becoming wildly popular, and it seems those who do this often prefer some sort of zero-magnification, red dot-style sight.

A wide variety of optical sights can be used for hog eradication or hunting. This Redfield Counter Strike is a prismatic sight with multiple color reticles and an integrated red laser.

SPORT AND RECREATION

The AR becomes more popular for competition and recreation every day, and there are a variety of competition disciplines where it is used successfully. It's almost impossible to identify one type of optical sight that would best suit an AR set up for competition or recreational shooting, due to the variety of the matches and shooting exercises. Still, common sense applies. For close range, red dot-style sights are popular, while, for close to moderate ranges, traditionally styled, variable powered optics with ballistic reticles are relatively predominate. As for long range, the same scope that might be used in a tactical, precision long-range scenario would work just fine.

A multitude of sights can be used for sport and recreational shooting. Simple in looks but rugged in construction, this Trijicon SRS reflex sight would be a fine choice.

BUT WHAT ARE THE DIFFERENCES IN ALL THESE OPTICAL SIGHTS?

Let's start with the red dots. There are essentially three different types of so-called red dot sights: holographic, prismatic, and reflex. They all help you put your bullets where you want and they all superimpose an

Red dot sights can be either very affordable and very expensive. This Tactical Reflex Sight from Cabela's sells for less than $200.

illuminated aiming point over your field of view, but they are all not the same thing.

The term "red dot" has morphed into a term to describe any compact, zero or low magnification optical sight with an illuminated aiming point. Kind of like how the word "Coke" is often used to describe any cola. Asking for a red dot sight is kind of like asking for a Coke. The waitress might respond, "Is Pepsi okay?" while the guy behind the gun store counter might say, "Is a holo-sight okay?"

RED DOT /REFLEX SIGHTS

True red dot sights are actually reflex sights. The aiming point or dot is an LED (light emitting diode) projected forward onto a lens. The lens is kind of like a mirror, and, because of that, the optical brightness of the image you see when looking through the sight is slightly darker than with a standard rifle scope, holographic, or prismatic sight. There are essentially two styles of reflex

300 BLK Zero

Subsonic | Supersonic

50 yd   100 yd

150 yd   300 yd

The reticle in this EOTech sight offers trajectory compensation for subsonic and supersonic .300 AAC Blackout loads.

Holographic sights allow both-eyes-open shooting, just like reflex sights, but, due to their design, they can have complex, trajectory compensating reticles. This EOTech XPS 300 holographic sight was made just for the .300 AAC Blackout cartridge.

sights. One is very compact and L-shaped and the other is tube-shaped, similar to a conventional rifle scope. Red dot sights vary a great deal in price.

HOLOGRAPHIC SIGHTS

A holographic sight or "holo-sight," as it is often called, has a photograph of a reticle sandwiched between layers of glass. A laser projected onto the glass illuminates the reticle. Since the reticle is a hologram, it can be in any shape. At this time, EOTech is the only company manufacturing holographic firearms sights.

PRISMATIC SIGHTS

The prismatic red dot sight is similar to a rifle scope, although they have fewer lenses. What a prismatic red dot does have is a prism to flip the image so it does not appear upside down. In a prismatic sight, the reticle is etched on glass, so it can be in any shape or configuration. It can also be illuminated. Unlike reflex and holographic sights that have no eye relief constraints, a prismatic sight will have a set eye relief similar to that of a traditional rifle scope. Prismatic sights are generally not very expensive.

Though bulkier than reflex sights, prismatic sights can be less expensive. However, they are dependent on a set eye relief.

Regardless the type, these sights are popular for AR-style rifles and carbines for several reasons. Whether in sport shooting, personal protection, or hunting environments, many ARs are employed at very close to moderate ranges, where no to low magnification and an easy to see reticle shine. Many of these sights can also be co-witnessed with iron sights and used in conjunction with night vision devices. Also, to an extent, their popularity is a result of military adoption, and civilian consumers do tend to follow the military's lead.

Red dots have also become affordable. Understandably, you may not be able to drop the grand necessary to pick up the latest Trijicon reflex sight being used by some super-secret, ninja-like military unit, but there are red dot options available for only a couple hundred bucks.

TRADITIONAL RIFLE SCOPES

Traditional rifle scopes are less complicated than the red dot styles and most shooters are familiar with them. Most do not need batteries to function, and their magnifications can vary from slightly more than 1x to 36x or more. Unlike true red dot and holographic sights, traditional rifle scopes have a set eye relief; that means your eye must be positioned within a range of about three to five inches behind the ocular lens for you to get a full sight picture through the scope.

Prices can vary on traditional rifle scopes from $100 to $2,000 dollars. Some say that, with rifle scopes, you get what you pay for. That may very well be true. However, once you get above a price of about $500, the differences in quality and serviceability become smaller and smaller.

Target turrets are a common feature on precision, long-range tactical rifle scopes. They allow for quick and precise adjustment to compensate for bullet drop, wind, and other atmospheric conditions.

Tactical, traditionally styled rifle scopes are generally represented by two types of optical sights. One style has a low magnification range and the other will have a moderately high magnification range. Both are typically equipped with a special purpose reticle designed to compensate for bullet drop and/or to be used to range targets of a specific size, like maybe the torso of an enemy combatant.

Easy to access target turrets are also a common element of a tactical rifle scope. They allow the shooter to make swift and accurate adjustments to the reticle to compensate for distance and wind, as well as a variety of other atmospheric conditions.

Due to the way the AR platform is configured, high scope mounting is the norm. Because of this, high rings or special AR mounting systems are desirable.

Leupold, Talley, Trijicon, Warne, and a variety of other companies manufacture rings specifically for mounting traditional rifle scopes to the Picatinny rail found on flat-top AR upper receivers.

Tactical rifle scopes can be affordable or insanely expensive, with some at the higher end costing as much as three grand.

MOUNTS, BASES, AND RINGS

No matter what type optical sight you choose, you will have to mount it to your AR. Most of the true red dot, holographic, and prismatic sights come with integral mounting systems built into the sight. Traditional and tactical rifle scopes will need, at a minimum, rings that can be attached to the rail on top of your AR's upper receiver. One-piece mount systems that offer quick-detach capability are starting to emerge, and these greatly simplify the mounting process. Such quick-detach units typically position the scope at the correct height above the bore for proper alignment with your eye, too.

PROPER SCOPE MOUNTING

Mounting a red dot-style sight with an integral mounting system is very easy, and everything is preset from the factory, so that the sight goes on square and level. All you'll need to worry about is positioning the sight to address any issues that might result from the use of a magnifier, open sights, or the potential use of night vision optics. In the case of a prismatic sight, you will also need to address eye relief.

With a traditional scope, you need to be concerned with eye relief, but you also need to ensure the scope is level. This can be a trial by error exercise with a traditional rifle, but, with the AR, it's easy. You can use two small levels such as those supplied with the Weaver scope mounting tool kit, or you can vise your AR and adjust the vise so that the rail on top of the upper receiver is level.

This IMS (Integral Mount System) from Leupold was designed specifically for mounting a traditional rifle scope to the flat-top Picatinny rail on an AR.

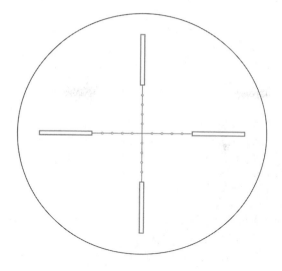

The Mil-Dot reticle features additional aiming points or references, which are spaced equal distances apart.

Then, when you install the scope, place a level on the top of the vertical adjustment turret and make sure it's even. If your scope isn't level, the problem will be evidenced at longer ranges, as the bullet will not drop directly under the point of aim. It will land below and to the left or right of center.

Everything needs to be tight on your optics mount, but not too tight. Over torquing scope rings and base screws is common and can lead to scope damage and failure. As a general rule, you should torque scope rings to between 20 and 25 foot-pounds (ft-lbs) and base screws to 30 ft-lbs. A torque wrench is handy for scope mounting and not a bad tool to have around in general, if you own an AR.

Zeroing or sighting in your optical sight is covered in Chapter 12, but prior to sighting in, it's always a good idea to bore sight. To bore sight, vise the detached upper receiver with the optical sight attached, or rest your setup on sandbags. Look down the bore and position the upper receiver so that a spot at least 50 yards downrange is centered in the bore. Now, adjust the optical sight so that the aiming point is centered over this spot. You should be able to look through the bore, raise your head and look through the sight, and see the exact same spot centered in both. Note

that this is *not* the same as sighting in your AR, but it will get you close and potentially save some time and ammo on the range.

A NOTE ON BALLISTIC RETICLES

Ballistic reticles have become almost standard equipment on optical sights. Once relegated to only a few traditional rifle scopes, ballistic reticles are appearing in almost every type of rifle scope and even holographic and prismatic sights. Early ballistic reticles tended to be generic, meaning they were designed to work with a wide range of cartridges. Newer ballistic reticles are now designed to work with only a single, specific cartridge or load.

There are essentially two types of ballistic reticles. The first and oldest is the Mil-Dot reticle, which has multiple aiming points positioned below the center of the reticle. These additional aiming points are spaced at equal distances apart. Mil-Dot reticles also have these graduations on the horizontal crosswire and on the vertical wire above reticle center. To use a Mil-Dot reticle properly, you need to know the needed correction in Mils (milliradians of angle, different than MOA, or minute of angle), for your ammo at each distance.

M-223 2-8x32

BDC 600			
	8x		8x
A	0.25	K	8.25
B	8	L	10.25
C	0.5	M	12.5
D	1	N	14.75
E	0.75	O	17
F	1.5	P	1
G	2.5		
H	3.75		
I	5		
J	6.5		

This diagram and reference chart for the Nikon M223 BDC 600 reticle show the exact subtension for each reference point on the reticle at 100 yards. This reticle was designed for the .223 Remington cartridge and is standard in the Nikon P 223 rifle scope.

There are other takes on the Mil-Dot concept where, instead of dots or hash marks along the crosswires, there's a complex grid that's used the same way. Additionally, there are MOA reticles, where the dots or hash marks are separated by minutes of angle (as opposed to Mils) or $1/10$-Mils. Actually, the variations on the Mil-Dot concept are many, but what they all have in common is that the marks or additional aiming points are separated by the same distance, or "subtend" to the same distance. Subtension describes the measurement the space between these aiming points equals at different ranges. If you increase the range to the target, the subtension is increased proportionally. For example, one Mil equals 3.6 inches at 100 yards. At 200 yards, then, it will equal 7.2 inches.

Modern ballistic reticles take the math out of the equation. The subtension of the additional aiming points below reticle center correlate with the estimated or projected drop of the bullet at a certain distance. For example, a reticle may be engineered to match the trajectory of the .223 Remington, when firing a common 55-grain bullet moving at 3,240 fps. In this case, the first additional aiming point might subtend to eight inches at 300 yards and the second aiming point to 21 inches at 400 yards.

The problem with ballistic reticles is that they are based on generalities, not specifics. In other words, you're kind of guessing with one. Variations in velocity, altitude, and the atmospheric conditions will alter the trajectory of a bullet, so, no matter how precise the manufacturer's calculations when it engineered its ballistic reticle, it cannot be perfect. It might be close enough, but it will never *perfectly* match your bullets trajectory.

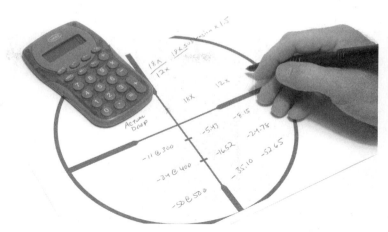

By working with a ballistics program and the actual drop of your ammo as verified on the range, you can tune your ballistic reticle to almost perfectly match the trajectory of at least one load—almost.

Choosing an optical sight can be as difficult as selecting your AR. The options are nearly endless. The great thing about the AR and its modern optics mounting systems is that you can have multiple optical sights and even swap between them as your heart desires, in most cases without having to re-zero either sight. So don't think you have to restrict or confine yourself to only one sight.

I asked combat veteran and Magpul employee Cody Carroll his thoughts on optics for the AR. Here's some great advice from someone who has as they say, seen the elephant:

I have had the opportunity to work with a wide variety of optics on the AR platform in both combat and training throughout my career. I have found that today's offerings of low-powered variable optics are superb choices for a variety of shooter tasks. The glass has to be of high quality, and it should offer an illuminated dot or circle for close-in, time-sensitive engagements. I also want a simple Mil-based reticle, and turrets that also adjust in milliradian increments, to eliminate the need for reticle-to-turret conversion calculations.

I have found that the a second focal plane reticle usually works best for me with these

low-powered optics, because the more complicated first focal plane reticles graduated in .2 Mils are indistinguishable to my eye at low power. I have also found the second focal plane reticle ideal for fast-moving aerial platform shooting, as you can still use the full reticle with holds on the lowest power setting (though it does take some work to figure out what the reticle increments work out to on different magnification settings).

Super Soldier Cody Carroll, Force Reconnaissance Marine and Magpul Industries Product Manager.

CHAPTER 8

COMMON-SENSE AR ACCESSORIES

With the AR, it is an almost incomprehensible task to list the accessories available. Aftermarket options exist for almost every single part, and upgrades and add-ons are available for each major component, to include the stock, lower receiver, upper receiver, handguard, and barrel. It would take a book—no, *volumes*—to even attempt to list the available options. Not only that, by the time you got the book published, it would be antiquated, because new accessories are being introduced every day, and new companies are being formed to offer AR accessories almost as quickly. It's almost like the AR is a computer—buy or read about one today and tomorrow things have changed.

All that said, you can see why the task of talking about or listing accessories might be the most difficult of all, when it comes to a comprehensive look at the AR. So let's consider the most common modifications generally made to an AR and work from there.

TRIGGERS

It's no secret that Mil Spec AR triggers are terrible. They have everything a good trigger does not have, like take-up, creep, over-travel, and inconsistency. Because of this, a number of manufacturers offer aftermarket triggers for the AR-15 and the AR-10. (As a side note, triggers for the AR-10 and AR-15 are different and are, therefore, not interchangeable.) I could recommend most any of these triggers, but, more importantly, let me explain to you what a good trigger actually is.

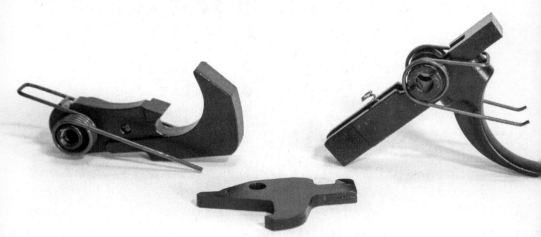

Mil Spec AR triggers are notorious for being terrible. If you make only one upgrade to your AR, replace the Mil Spec trigger.

When we are born, we enter a life of buttons and switches, those many things that must be pulled, pushed, or flipped in order for us to get what we want. From a metaphorical standpoint, we push these buttons and pull these strings of life in many ways. From turning on the radio in our car to the subtle looks we give our significant others, we are flipping switches.

It is no different when we shoot. To make our rifles fire, we must pull the trigger. However, when compared to the other buttons we physically manipulate, pulling a trigger is more akin to that wink you give to get a kiss. Pulling a trigger is a much more subtle exercise than jabbing at a light switch or poking the TV remote. When you pull a trigger you have—hopefully—ended your hunt,

stopped a threat, or hit dead center of your target. Pulling a trigger might be one of the ultimate exercises in hand/eye coordination.

What we simply cannot do is shoot a rifle with precision, if it has a bad trigger. The really sad thing is that most shooters do not know what a good trigger really is—and just because a rifle is expensive doesn't mean it has a good trigger. I test dozens of ARs every year and have done so for a long time. The percentage of those rifles that come with a good trigger is less than 10.

A trigger is a moving mechanism, and there are several terms used to describe how it moves. It's important to understand both the movement and the terms, so you can evaluate a trigger and better understand how to pull one. Following are the common terms used

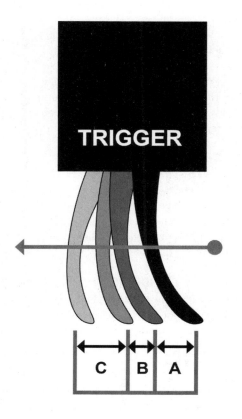

TRIGGER MOVEMENT

A = Take-up. This is the distance the trigger moves prior to meeting resistance.

B = Creep. This is the distance the trigger moves after resistance has been felt.

C = Over-Travel. This is the distance the trigger moves after the sear has been released.

to describe trigger function. Let's define each separately and examine how their function can negatively or positively impact your shooting.

TAKE-UP

Take-up describes the initial movement of a trigger before resistance is met. There are two types of triggers, single-stage and two-stage. Both can have take-up, but, with a two-stage trigger, you'll feel some resistance, which can be as much as half the overall pull weight, during take-up. Take-up with a single-stage trigger is generally very light and is completed over an infinitesimal distance. In other words, a good single-stage trigger has no take-up; you put your finger on it, apply pressure, and the rifle goes bang.

PULL WEIGHT

Pull weight describes the amount of pressure that must be applied to a trigger to release the sear. Pull weight can vary a great deal, and shooters often argue about what an ideal pull weight should be. Here again we are talking about *feel,* so opinions are subjective.

A good place to start is with a pull weight that is no more than half the weight of the rifle itself. The reason for this should be obvious. If you have pressure to the trigger that equals or exceeds the rifle's weight, how are you supposed to keep your sights on target without moving the rifle?

CREEP

Creep describes the movement of a trigger after take-up but prior to sear release. Creep is very common in factory triggers. Know that you can have a trigger with very minimal creep and still shoot with precision as long as the creep is smooth and consistent. It is in experiencing trigger creep that you will often feel roughness and inconsistency. This is due to the wide tolerances found in the mass-produced and inexpensive parts that make up many factory trigger mechanisms.

OVER-TRAVEL

The importance of over-travel is probably the most misunderstood aspect of a trigger. Over-travel relates to the movement of the trigger after the sear has been released. Very few triggers have no over-travel, but a good trigger will have very little or an almost imperceivable amount.

Why is over-travel so important? As hard as it may seem to believe—considering that bullets leave rifle barrels sometimes in excess of 3,000 fps—the movement of your finger on the trigger after the sear has been released can move the rifle before the bullet exists the barrel. The flight time of most bullets through a rifle barrel is between 1.0 and 1.5 milliseconds. The "lock time," the time between sear release and primer ignition, can be five times that long. Any movement to the rifle prior to the bullet exiting the barrel will affect your point of impact and excessive over-travel will cause this movement. Due to the higher force imparted on the trigger when it stops, a heavy pull weight will exaggerate the effects of over-travel. In essence, what you're doing when you pull a trigger with excessive over-travel is inducing movement to your launch platform. It's kind of like you're trying to throw a curve ball.

CONSISTENCY

Consistency is probably the most important aspect of any trigger, regardless its pull weight, creep, take-up, or over-travel. This consistency is why companies like Timney Triggers are in business.

REPLACEMENT TRIGGERS

Now, with some understanding of what a good trigger should feel like, you can start experimenting with triggers to see which ones pull in a manner that pleases you and will lead to good shooting. Triggers are relatively easy to install on an AR, and most installations can be accomplished in about 15 minutes.

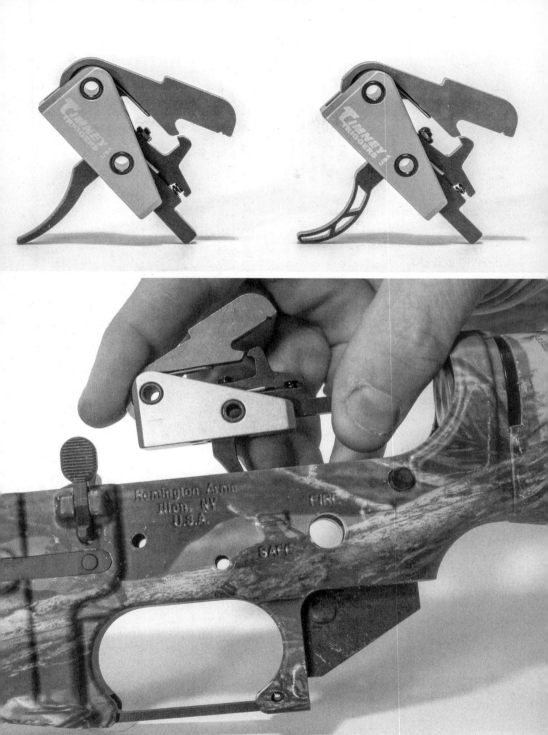

Aftermarket AR triggers like those from Timney are relatively easy to install. The complete process can be finished in about 15 minutes.

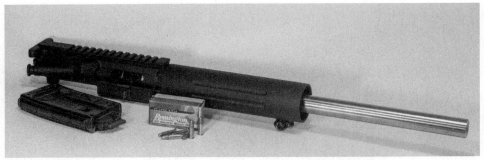

This DPMS dedicated .22 LR upper receiver will turn your AR into a rimfire in seconds.

UPPER RECEIVERS

As you will learn, as you continue through this book, one of the main aspects of the AR's versatility is how easily and quickly upper receivers can be switched. Many companies manufacturer upper receivers for ARs that will allow you to convert your AR so that it will fire a different cartridge. And, as we've seen, there are a lot of cartridges that can be fired in the AR.

One common and very useful upper receiver upgrade is one that will allow you to fire .22 LR ammo. The importance of this should be obvious; it allows you to practice with *your* trigger and *your* AR for a fraction of the cost it takes to fire centerfire cartridges.

Aside from the multitude of centerfire upper receivers that can be installed on an AR lower receiver, you can also get an upper from Crosman that will turn your AR into an air gun that will shoot .177-caliber pellets. Tell me another weapon system that will allow you to do that?

Additional uppers and triggers seem to be the most common major upgrades associated with the AR, but there are countless other trinkets, gadgets and, yes, even very useful add-ons you can attach. As mentioned, it would take volumes to list them all, but the best way for you to find what's available is to probably go to www.brownells.com and utilize its AR Builder web feature to explore these many options.

ALL THE OTHER STUFF: ONE GREAT EXAMPLE

Magpul Industries is a designer and manufacturer of polymer firearms accessories, primarily for the AR. It established a stellar reputation for the exquisite AR magazines it produces. Many consider the Magpul P-Mag to be the best AR-15 magazine available. Struggling with how to present the world of AR accessories, it seemed logical to just

What other weapon system can go from a .223 Remington to a .22 LR and to a pellet rifle in seconds? This complete upper from Crosman allows you to shoot airgun pellets from your AR!

The Magpul MOE stock is one of the most popular collapsible AR stocks on the market.

Magpul offers a variety of collapsible AR stocks. The ACS is just one of the many.

Magpul also offers fixed stocks. One is non-adjustable and the other has an adjustable cheek piece and is modifiable for length of pull.

The Magpul RAS QD and RSA sling attachments attach directly to the handguard via a Picatinny rail.

take a snapshot of what this one company, Magpul Industries, has to offer the shooter who wants to upgrade, modify, improve, or otherwise trick out their AR. Here are some of the common AR additions available from Magpul. Understand that similar and very different versions of all of these parts can be purchased from a wide variety of other manufacturers.

STOCKS

The original AR stock was a hollow, fiberglass, fixed stock, but the adjustable buttstock has supplanted the A1-style stock as the most popular version employed today. Magpul offers a variety of adjustable stocks. In fact, it offers six different collapsible buttstocks, the MOE, CTR, STR, ACS-L, ACS, and the UBR. Magpul also offers a fixed-position stock that is adjustable for length of pull and also comes with an adjustable cheek piece.

Magpul's ASAP single-point sling attachment goes between the buttstock and the lower receiver.

SLINGS AND SLING ATTACHMENTS

Many recreational shooters do not install a sling on their AR. Those who hunt with ARs or who use them in tactical applications, on the other hand, wouldn't dream of *not* having a sling.

There are basically two ways to attach a sling to an AR. It can be attached at the two locations you would find on a traditional rifle, or it can be attached at a single location. Interestingly, many modern ARs do not

The Magpul Multi-Mission single-point sling will work with any single-point sling attachment. It can also be converted to work as a dual attachment point sling.

Like many other companies, Magpul offers detachable AR sights. Its polymer MBUS sights (far left) are very popular. The PRO version rear (left) and front sights (two right) are a steel rendition of the MBUS.

come with sling attachments beyond those normally incorporated in the buttstock.

Magpul offers the RSA and the RSA QD rail sling attachments. These units clamp onto a section of Picatinny or Mil Spec rail and provide a hoop for the attachment of a sling. Generally, these sling attachments are applied to a handguard and are used with a sling that has two attachment points.

Magpul also offers what it calls the Ambidextrous Sling Attachment Point (ASAP). This device is installed between the buttstock and the lower receiver. It is specifically engineered to work with a single-point sling.

When it comes to slings with dual attachment points, about any common rifle sling will work, though many companies offer dual attachment point slings specifically designed for the AR. Still, the most common AR sling is the single-point sling. Magpul's take on this sling is called the MS3 Multi-Mission Sling. With this one you get more than you pay for, because it can be converted to work as a dual-point sling.

SIGHTS

Sights for the AR were covered in a previous chapter, but the Magpul MBUS (Magpul Back-Up Sights) deserve mention here, because they have become standard equipment on many factory ARs. This is

due to the sights' low profile when folded out of the way, as well as their ruggedness and cost. Magpul also offers a Pro version of the MBUS front and rear sight, which is a corrosion-resistant, all-steel model.

HANDGUARDS

Magpul does not offer a wide selection of handguards, but it does offer carbine-, mid-, and rifle-length versions of its MOE (Magpul Original Equipment) handguard. As it is with the Magpul MBUS Sights, the MOE handguard and MOE buttstock have both become popular as original equipment on rifles from a variety of manufacturers like Bushmaster and Smith & Wesson.

Magpul's standard MOE handguard is very popular with many manufacturers and is available in carbine-, mid-, and rifle-length versions.

This Mossberg MMR has a tubular handguard. Designed as a hunting rifle, there is not as much need for rails to allow the attachment of tactical type devices. It is very comfortable in hand.

Let's, for a moment, step away from the Magpul advertisement—no, it's not really an advertisement, but, when one company makes so many AR accessories that have been proven to work, that company and its products needs to be recognized—and discuss other handguards. There are two very common variations. The first would be the quad-rail handguard, which is a free-floating handguard with integral rails on the top, bottom, and both sides. These are available from a variety of manufactures and are popular because they allow you to install accessories at any point along the handguard. The other very popular handguard is the tubular handguard. One complaint with the quad-rail handguard is that it is not very comfortable

to hold. As an answer to that, the tubular handguard is nothing more than a section of aluminum tubing. Most have pre-drilled holes to allow for the installation of rail sections, and most also have some sort of texture, to them to help make your grip solid.

The latest handguard type beginning to get a lot of traction is something of a cross between a quad-rail handguard and a tubular handguard. These handguards may be more square in shape, but have radiused edges to make them more comfortable to hold. They also have a multitude of pre-drilled screw holes, to allow for the attachment of rail sections. Some even come with pre-drilled holes that will accept quick-detach sling swivels.

This Wilson Combat T.R.I.M. (Tactical Rail Interface Modular) handguard is representative of the modern AR handguard. It is comfortable to hold onto and is also adaptable to rail sections.

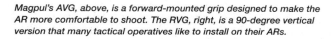

Magpul's AVG, above, is a forward-mounted grip designed to make the AR more comfortable to shoot. The RVG, right, is a 90-degree vertical version that many tactical operatives like to install on their ARs.

FORE-GRIPS AND HAND GRIPS

Many AR shooters like the idea and feel of a vertical fore-grip that can be mounted to the handguard of the AR. For some, these vertical fore-grips are more comfortable to hold on to, particularly in tactical applications. The Magpul RVG attaches to a section of rail on the underside of the handguard and provides a 90-degree vertical fore-grip. Magpul also offers the AFG, which is an angled fore-grip. It attaches in the same manner, but, instead of offering a 90-degree fore-grip, this unit provides a grip at about a 30- to 40-degree angle.

With regards to the pistol grip on the AR, Magpul, like a number of companies, has more than a half-dozen to choose from. The simplest is the MOE-K grip, which doesn't look much different than the common AR grip. Its MIAD Gen 1.1 Grip Kit, on the other hand, is a modular grip similar to those found on some of the newer polymer handguns. The MIAD grip allows the user to change the front and rear backstrap on the grip to perfectly suit the individual hand.

Another fore-grip that needs mentioning is the Crimson Trace Modular Vertical Fore-grip (MVF.) This unit, like the Magpul RVG,

The MOE-K pistol grip from Magpul (left) is simple in design and very similar to a common AR grip. Conversely, the company's MIAD grip (right) allows the user to customize how the grip feels in their hand.

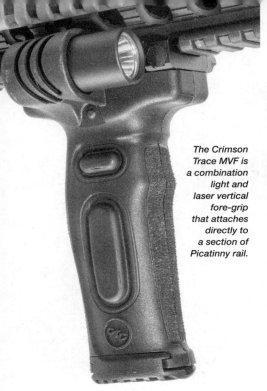

The Crimson Trace MVF is a combination light and laser vertical fore-grip that attaches directly to a section of Picatinny rail.

This Lehigh Defense suppressor will work on any .22- or .30-caliber rifle, as long as the correct attachment or adapter is used. With multiple adapters, you could use these suppressors on ARs and/or bolt-action rifles.

attaches to a section of rail on the underside of the handguard, but this one also has a built-in light and laser. Both are accessories that have wide tactical application, and they can even be used in many hunting scenarios where hunting at night is legal.

SUPPRESSORS

Sound suppressors are becoming a very popular AR accessory. Tactical operatives, hunters, and even recreational and sport shooters now use them regularly. They do not make an AR or any firearm silent, but, with supersonic ammo, the noise is greatly reduced. With subsonic ammo, they are indeed very quiet. The last chapter in this book deals with legalities, and there you can find additional information about owning a suppressor, but let's look at the tools themselves here.

Suppressors vary in size, style, and function. You can get them just for subsonic or supersonic use, and some are rated for both. You can also get a suppressor that will stand up to high-volume—fully automatic—fire.

The ways suppressors attach to the AR will vary. Some suppressors will screw di-

This .30-caliber Surefire suppressor will work on a .30-caliber AR and even on a .22-caliber AR. However, the noise reduction on the smaller-caliber AR will not be as great. Surefire offers a quick-attachment solution for suppressors that will prevent thread damage and make the installation and removal process much faster.

Magpul offers baseplates for your AR magazines that make them easy to remove from a mag pouch or that will protect them when they hit the ground.

rectly onto the threads on the muzzle of the AR where the flash hider is attached. Others work in conjunction with a flash hider by utilizing a proprietary locking device, and some of these, like those from Surefire, offer quick on and off. You can install or remove these suppressors in a matter of seconds.

Suppressors are not inexpensive, so it's a good idea to do some research and find a versatile unit that might work on more than one of your ARs or AR uppers, as well as one that can function on other rifles.

Magpul and many other companies offer sections of Picatinny rail that can be attached to various handguards via screws. These rail sections allow you to mount a wide range of accessories.

THERE'S MORE?

What else can you attach to your AR? Well, let's see.

There are followers for your magazines designed to make them more reliable. There are also baseplates that can be attached to your magazines to protect them or to make them easier to remove or pull from a magazine carrier. There are buttpads and cheekpieces for buttstocks, and little rubber ladder-looking do-dads for rail sections to make them less aggressive on your hands. There are innumerable lights, lasers, and light/laser combination devices that can be installed on an AR, as well as all sorts of other bells and whistles. If you think there is something that should be attached to your AR, there is probably a device to do that. There is very likely even a device that will attach things to your AR that should never be attached to it. The list does indeed go on.

Magpul even offers complete training DVDs for those interested in how to manipulate, operate, and shoot their AR.

CHAPTER 9

MANUAL OF ARMS

Before handling or shooting any firearm without supervision, it is a great idea to understand the manual of arms for that particular firearm. In other words, you need to know how to unload and clear it, load it, and perform immediate action. At the risk of being too basic, let's define each of these actions.

UNLOAD/CLEAR

To clear a firearm, you verify two things, first, that there is no cartridge in the chamber and, second, that a source of ammunition is not attached to the gun. The act of clearing an AR (or any firearm) is the same process used to unload the firearm. After adhering to a total understanding and dedication to the four rules of firearms safety (below), this is the second-most critical part of the manual of arms and of owning, operating, and shooting any firearm.

LOAD

Loading a firearm involves three actions: making sure that the firearm is clear, inserting a source of ammunition into it, and chambering a cartridge. The loading process should be committed to memory and followed in steps, just like unloading and clearing. You cannot shoot your AR if it is not loaded, so this becomes the third-most critical part of the manual of arms.

GUN RULES TO LIVE BY

Rule No. 1: All guns are always loaded.
Well, no, not really. Some guns are unloaded. The thing is, if we *treat* all guns as if they are loaded, the less likely we are to do stupid things with them like pointing them at ourselves, our wives, our kids, and others. Just like you often read in the paper or hear on the news, a husband shoots wife and then says, "I thought the gun was unloaded."
Rule No. 2: Never let the muzzle cover anything you are not willing to destroy.
If there were only one rule of gun safety, this would be it. In fact, it is the first rule I teach and the one rule I demand 100-percent compliance with. If gun owners followed this single safety rule for their rest of eternity, the blind would be the only ones perpetuating accidental deaths and injuries related to the discharge of a firearm.
Rule No. 3: Keep your finger off the trigger until your sights are on the target.
Why would you do this? Simple, to make sure you don't inadvertently pull the trigger when you are not ready.
Rule No. 4. Always be sure of your target.
What does this mean? It means you only shoot at things that are okay to shoot at. Can you shoot at paper targets? Sure. But, be careful about what is beyond them, between you and them, and to your flanks.

IMMEDIATE ACTION

This is the action taken by you to correct a stoppage. A stoppage is when a malfunction of the gun, ammunition, or operator puts the gun in a condition where it will not fire. Sometimes a stoppage is referred to as a "jam."

Now, with an understanding of what a manual of arms is, we can look how to properly perform each of these tasks. Practice these steps before you go to the range unsupervised, so that you intimately familiar with them.

UNLOAD/CLEAR

Anytime you pick up an AR, the first thing you should do is to make sure it is unloaded and clear. There is a process for doing this:

1. With the AR pointed in a safe direction and on SAFE and with your shooting hand firmly grasping the pistol grip, depresses the magazine release with your trigger finger.
2. Catch the magazine with your support hand, as it is ejected from the AR.

Depress the magazine release and remove the magazine.

3. Secure the ejected magazine in a pocket or dump pouch.
4. Grasp the AR around the magazine well with your support hand, with the palm of your support hand on the magazine well, your fingers in front of and on the side of the magazine well, and your support hand thumb hovering over the bolt lock/release.

Pull the charging handle to the rear. This will extract and eject a cartridge from the chamber.

5. Move your shooting hand from the pistol grip to the charging handle with your thumb or index finger positioned over the release on the left side of the charging handle.
6. Pull the charging handle to the rear. You may find this easier to do if you position the stock of the AR on your chest.
7. Retract the charging handle completely to the rear. If there is a cartridge in the chamber, this should extract it and cause it to be ejected from the AR. Let the cartridge fall to the ground; do not attempt to catch it.
8. Allow the charging handle to go forward, then fully retract it two more times.
9. After you have pulled the charging handle to the rear for the third time, hold it to the rear and depress the bolt lock with the thumb of your left hand. Then push the charging handle forward, allowing it to lock in place.

10. At this time, the AR should be unloaded and clear, but you need to make sure. Visually inspect the magazine well and the chamber and then physically inspect them both by inserting your fingers into both.

With the charging handle pulled to the rear, depress the bolt lock with the thumb on your left hand. This will lock the bolt open.

Return the charging handle to the forward position.

An AR should never be considered to be unloaded and clear until these 10 steps have been performed. Once you are confident the AR is unloaded and clear, sling it or place it on the bench. Then and only then should you recover ejected cartridges from the ground.

LOAD

There are three ways to load an AR, administratively, via a speed load, or via a

Visually and physically inspect the chamber to ensure the AR is unloaded.

tactical load. An administrative load is used during informal shooting and when zeroing or testing the AR, sights, optics, or ammunition. A speed load is conducted anytime you need to get a fully loaded magazine into a rifle that has a less than fully loaded magazine installed. A speed load can also be performed if the bolt on the AR has been locked to the rear as a result of expending all the ammunition that had been in the magazine. As the name suggests, a speed load is performed when time is of the essence. Finally, a tactical load is performed when time is not an issue, perhaps while hunting or even during a lull in a firefight. With a tactical reload, you are replacing a magazine that is not fully loaded with one that is, but, the tactical reload allows you to maintain control of the partially loaded magazine you remove from the AR. Let's look at the steps required to perform each.

ADMINISTRATIVE LOAD
1. Make sure the AR is unloaded and clear, that the AR is pointed in a safe direction, and that the safety is in the safe position.
2. Secure a loaded magazine from a magazine pouch, table, or shooting bench. Feel and/or visually inspect the magazine to verify that the top round is firmly seated to the rear of the magazine. You should also make note of the side of the magazine on which the top round in positioned.
3. Holding the pistol grip of the AR with

Secure a loaded magazine in your support hand.

your shooting hand, insert a loaded magazine into the magazine well until you feel it lock in place.

Insert the loaded magazine into the AR.

4. Pull on the magazine with your support hand to verify that it is locked in place.
5. With the palm of your support hand, slap the bolt lock/release on the left side of the AR. This will release the bolt and allow it to move forward to chamber the top cartridge in the magazine.
6. Grab the magazine with your support hand and depress the magazine release with your trigger finger. This will cause the magazine to be ejected form the AR.
7. Visually and/or physically inspect the top of the magazine to determine the side of the magazine on which the top round is now positioned. If, when you first inserted the magazine into the AR, the top cartridge was positioned on the left side, and if the bolt actually chambered a cartridge, the top round on the magazine should now be positioned on the right side of the magazine.

8. Confirming that a cartridge was chambered, firmly reinsert the magazine into the magazine well.

(Above) Secure a fully loaded magazine with your support hand.

(Above) Eject the magazine in the AR and let it fall to the ground.

(Below and bottom) It is important to secure the magazine properly in your hand, so that you may also use that hand to remove the partially expended magazine in the AR.

9. With your support hand, pull down on the magazine to ensure it is locked in place.

SPEED LOAD

1. With the AR pointed in a safe direction and with your shooting hand grasping the pistol grip, retrieve a fully loaded magazine with your support hand.
2. Depress the magazine release with your trigger finger and allow the magazine that is in the AR to fall to the ground.
3. Insert the new magazine firmly into the magazine well with your support hand.
4. Pull down the on the magazine to ensure it is locked in place.
5. With your support hand, slap the bolt lock/release. Note: you might conduct a speed load before you have exhausted the ammunition supply in the magazine that is in the AR. If this is the case, the bolt will be forward and a cartridge will still be in the chamber of the AR. The alternative, of course, is that you will conduct a speed load after you have exhausted the ammo supply that is in the magazine in the AR. If this is the case, the bolt should be locked to the rear. In either case, slapping the bolt lock/release will ensure that the bolt is forward before you attempt to continue engaging targets.

TACTICAL RELOAD

1. With the AR pointed in a safe direction and with your shooting hand grasping the pistol grip, retrieve a fully loaded magazine with your support hand.
2. While holding the new magazine with your index finger and thumb wrapped around the base of the magazine, grab the magazine that is still in the AR, gripping it with the bottom three fingers on your support hand. Alternately, you can grasp the new magazine with your support hand like you would a pistol grip or a baseball bat. Either way, make sure

While holding the new magazine in your support hand, gain control of the magazine in the AR with that same hand.

Depress the magazine release, maintaining control the magazine being ejected from the AR.

to grab the magazine that's in the AR at its base.

3. Depress the magazine release with your trigger finger and allow the magazine in

Shift or rotate your hand so that you can insert the fresh magazine, always maintaining control of the partially expended and ejected magazine.

the AR to be released. Pull it from the magazine well.

4. Shift or rotate your support hand so that the new magazine is positioned vertically with the open end directly under the magazine well. Insert the new magazine into the magazine well firmly with your support hand.

5. Pull down the on the magazine to ensure it is locked in place.

6. Secure the magazine you removed from the AR in a pocket or dump pouch.

7. With your support hand, slap the bolt lock/release. Note: you might conduct a tactical load before you have exhausted the ammunition supply in the magazine that is in the AR. If this is the case, the bolt will be forward and a cartridge will still be in the chamber of the AR. If you conduct a tactical load after you have exhausted the ammo supply in the magazine in the AR, the bolt should be locked to the rear. In either case, slapping the bolt lock/release will ensure that the bolt is forward before you attempt to continue engaging targets.

IMMEDIATE ACTION

There are three types of stoppages with an AR and, therefore, there are three different types of immediate actions required to remedy them. While they are all very similar, they do have minute differences. It is important that you apply the proper immediate action to deal with the stoppage that has occurred. Note that once a stoppage is experienced, you should always perform a Type I stoppage immediate action as a default and until it is determined which level of stoppage you are dealing with.

TYPE I: FAILURE TO FIRE STOPPAGE

A magazine that was not fully seated can cause this type stoppage. So can a bad cartridge, one that failed to fire after the trigger was pulled, the hammer fell, and the firing pin impacted the primer. An indication that you have a Type I stoppage is when you pull the trigger and hear a click or the AR does not fire. Regardless the reason, you want to get your AR up and running again as soon as possible, so the response is the same.

1. While maintaining control of the AR by holding the pistol grip with your support hand, grab the magazine in the AR with your support hand.
2. Firmly *push* the magazine into the AR and then firmly *pull* on the magazine to verify it is locked in place.

A Type II stoppage is when a cartridge case becomes trapped between the bolt and the ejection port.

3. Roll or tilt the AR about 30 degrees to the right.
4. Grasp the charging handle with your support hand and pull or rack it all the way to the rear and release it. At this point, a Type I malfunction should be cleared and you can evaluate the situation and engage as needed.

An acronym you can use to remember the steps to clear a Type I stoppage is PPRR—push, pull, roll, and rack.

TYPE II: STOVEPIPE STOPPAGE

A Type II stoppage occurs when a fired cartridge case becomes trapped between the bolt and the ejection port. This can be caused by a weakly loaded cartridge or a dirty gun, though it might also be a symptom of another, more critical, mechanical problem.

A Type II stoppage can be cleared in the same manner as a Type I stoppage. By checking that the magazine is inserted and locked in place, rolling the AR to the right, and racking the charging handle and releasing it, you will have ensured the magazine is firmly seated, allowed the cartridge case trapped by the bolt to fall free, and you should have chambered another cartridge from the magazine in the process.

Make sure the magazine is firmly seated and locked into place.

Roll the AR to the right, then cycle the charging handle to clear the stoppage.

Some will suggest and even teach that you should use your support hand to sweep the cartridge case trapped by the bolt out of the way before you operate the charging handle. The only problem with this approach is that it wastes time and provides no advantage over the process for clearing a Type I stoppage.

TYPE III: DOUBLE-FEED STOPPAGE

A Type III stoppage is the worst. Commonly known as a double feed, it can happen if a full cartridge or a fired, empty case in the chamber fails to extract. This might happen if the extractor is broken, if the chamber is dirty, or if you have fired an over-pressured round. The result is that, when the bolt travels back forward in its normal operation (or during an immediate action maneuver), it tries to push another cartridge from the magazine into the already full chamber.

Note: Immediate action will not clear a Type III stoppage.

1. Grab the magazine well of the AR with your left hand as you would if you were attempting to unload the AR.
2. With your right hand, grab the charging handle and pull it all the way to the rear.
3. While holding the charging handle to the rear, depress the bolt lock/release with the thumb of your left hand.
4. Push the charging handle forward until it locks in place.
5. Place your right hand onto the pistol grip and gain control of the AR.
6. Remove your left hand from the magazine well and grab the magazine.
7. Depress the magazine release with your index finger.
8. Rip the magazine from the AR with your

Grab the magazine well of the AR with your left hand and retract the bolt all the way to the rear with your other hand. Then, depress the bolt lock with the thumb of your left hand.

left hand and let it fall to the ground or store it under your shooting arm.

9. Grab the charging handle with your left hand and pull it to the rear and release it three times. Note: You might have to again lock the bolt to the rear and use your other hand to clear the jammed cartridges from the magazine well or chamber of the AR.

10. Once the jam has been cleared, insert a fresh magazine.

11. Pull the charging handle to the rear and release. This should complete the process and leave you ready to shoot with a fully loaded magazine.

READY POSITIONS

A ready position is the position in which you have the AR while you are moving or preparing to shoot. You would also use one or the other of these ready positions while you were stalking an animal, while you were negotiating a competition course of fire, or maybe while you were clearing a building. With either of these ready posi-

It may be necessary to use your fingers to clear the stoppage from the AR.

Remove the magazine and let it fall to the ground or store it under your shooting arm.

tions, the muzzle is always kept pointed in a safe direction, your finger is off the trigger, and the AR is on SAFE.

OUTDOOR READY

The outdoor ready position is the most frequently used ready position. It is perfect for use on the range, on a competition course, or while hunting. With the outdoor ready position, the butt of the AR is on your shoulder and the AR is held in a firing position, but with the rifle's sights well below your line of sight. To engage a target, you simply raise the AR up to your eye, align the sights, and shoot.

When working with an AR in tight confines, the indoor ready position is the best one to use.

The outdoor ready position is the most frequently used ready position and is the best position to use when you have room to operate.

INDOOR READY

The indoor ready position is useful when working in tight spaces. Maybe you are moving down a hallway or are negotiating a thicket while hunting. As it is with the outdoor ready position, the butt of the AR is held in place on your shoulder and both hands have a firing grip on the AR. However, with the indoor ready position, the muzzle of the rifle is pointed towards the ground, just to the left of your support foot. If you need to engage a target, you simply swing the AR up to your line of sight, obtain the proper sight alignment, and shoot.

CHAPTER 10

MAINTENANCE

The AR is not a self-cleaning instrument. In fact, as we discovered in the section about impingement and piston systems, if your AR is an impingement-driven gun, then it kind of poops where it eats. As bad as this sounds, it's not all that terrible a thing. The AR is a very durable weapon system that can still run reliably, even if it is very dirty—but that doesn't mean they can be neglected.

The first maintenance question a new AR owner will probably have is how often or when should they clean their AR? This is indeed a good question, but the answer isn't all that simple. For example, I have several ARs and I shoot them regularly. Now, while "regular" is a descriptive term, it is not definitive. Regular to me is at least once per month. Regular for a Gunsite instructor might be once or twice per week.

If you were in the military like me, you cleaned your firearm or weapon system at the end of every range session. The resulting assumption by all the soldiers was that you clean a weapon after it has been fired, *every time*. I submit that this assumption is incorrect. In the military, the cleaning of your weapon after every firing event was primarily a training exercise. It was done so that you would learn how to clean it and learn that you should care for it.

A well-built and cared for AR should run through at least 500 rounds of ammunition without any issues and no maintenance at all, even in harsh conditions. So, let's say you go to the range today and fire 100 rounds and return home. You're planning on going back to the range tomorrow. Do you need to clean your AR? No. Is it okay to clean your AR? Sure.

What if you're not planning to return to the range until next weekend? Cleaning still isn't mandatory. Modern ammunition is non-corrosive. Still, if you live in a location where there is high humidity or you were shooting in wet or very dirty conditions, it is a good idea to at least field strip and wipe down your AR. Sure, your upper and lower receivers are aluminum and will not rust. However, many of the parts inside the AR are steel.

Let's say you're attending a shooting course where you might be shooting as much as 250 rounds per day over the period of a week. That's more than 1,000 rounds! Your AR might make it through all 1,000 rounds without ever seeing a rag or lubrication, but, you are there to learn, and you cannot learn with a gun that will not go bang, so the sensible approach would be to perform some maintenance throughout the week.

Now, let's assume you have purchased a new optical sight for your AR and you head to the range to sight it in. You fire about 10 shots to establish zero, and then fire the rest of the 20-round box of ammunition for verification. When you leave the range, you have no plans to return. You may shoot again in a week at a local match or you may wait as long as a few months until hunting season. You've only fired 20 rounds, so, from a functioning standpoint, your rifle does not need to be cleaned, but it doesn't mean it's not a good idea to perform at least some preventive maintenance.

One maintenance area that gets a lot of attention is the barrel. There are many different opinions on when and how often a barrel should be cleaned. There are also lots of different barrels; no two are the same. One barrel may start to show degradation in accuracy, due to copper and carbon fouling, after as few as 30 or 40 rounds have been fired. Others may fire hundreds if not thousands of rounds before accuracy suffers. Every AR will be different, and you will have to discover the particulars of yours on your own.

Here's the thing, the AR was designed to be a volume-fire weapon. It's your job to keep it running, to make sure it is free of corrosion, and to ensure all the parts are in working order. There are no set rules, when it comes to cleaning an AR, but let's establish some different levels of service for your AR and then look in detail at each one. You can use the chart below as a guide as to when to perform these different levels of maintenance.

SITUATION	MAINTENANCE
Before Shooting	Pre-Fire Inspection
After Shooting	Post-Fire Inspection
After 100 Rounds	Range Expedient Cleaning
After 300 Rounds	Detail Cleaning
After 500 Rounds	Complete Service

DISASSEMBLY

Before you can reliably inspect, clean, or service an AR, you must know how to take it apart and reassemble it. The AR is easy to disassemble and put back together; it was made that way, so soldiers could perform these actions in battlefield conditions without the use of any tools (well, at least without tools or implements they did not commonly carry). The following is a step by step guide to the disassembly and reassembly of an AR at the operator level (i.e., not a gunsmithing level).

1. Unload and clear. (Refer to Chapter 9)
2. Release the bolt by depressing the bolt lock/release.
3. Push the rear action pin from left to right.
4. Tilt the upper receiver away from the lower receiver to about a 30 to 40 degree angle.
5. Pull the charging handle about two inches to the rear.
6. Grasp the bolt carrier and remove it from the upper receiver.
7. Remove the charging handle from the upper receiver.
8. Push the front action pin from the left to the right.
9. Separate the upper receiver from the lower receiver.
10. Remove the firing pin retaining key from the bolt carrier.
11. Remove the firing pin from the bolt. It should fall free, when the bolt is held vertically.
12. Rotate the bolt cam pin 90 degrees and pull it from the bolt carrier.
13. Remove the bolt from the bolt carrier.
14. Remove the extractor retaining pin and extractor.
15. Depress the buffer retainer and remove the buffer and buffer spring.
16. Depressing the delta ring and separating the handguard halves from around the barrel can remove military-style

handguards from an AR. It is a good idea to do this to check the condition of the gas system. However, military-style handguards are no longer that popular or common, and the more modern, free-floating handguards do not lend themselves to easy removal. If your AR has a more modern handguard, consult the manufacturer's instructions for removal.

Separating the upper and lower receiver will allow you to access the bolt carrier.

After unloading and clearing, the AR's bolt should be locked back. It needs to be forward and in battery for disassembly. This is achieved by pushing the bolt lock/release.

Gently retract the charging handle. This will pull the bolt carrier to the rear, so you can grab on to it for removal.

When the rear action pin is pushed fully to the right, it will stop and be held in place.

A gun vise is nice to hold your AR in place during cleaning and maintenance, but isn't necessary. You are ultimately going to end up with three major parts: upper receiver, lower receiver, and bolt assembly.

Ultimately, you need to remove the bolt from the bolt carrier, but, to do this, the bolt carrier must be removed from the upper receiver.

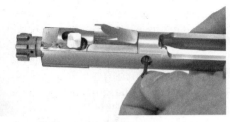

To remove the firing pin retaining key, you may need needle-nose pliers or a sharp object. It's also a good idea to have several of these pins on hand. Sometimes the used ones are hard to reinstall.

There is a slot in the upper receiver that will allow you to pull the charging handle from the upper receiver. Retract the charging handle until the tabs at the front line up with this slot.

By pushing the front action pin to the right, you can now separate the upper and lower receivers.

Unless the bolt assembly is very dirty, the firing pin should drop free after the retaining key has been removed.

196: To remove the bolt cam pin, the head of the pin will need to be positioned long-ways with the bolt.

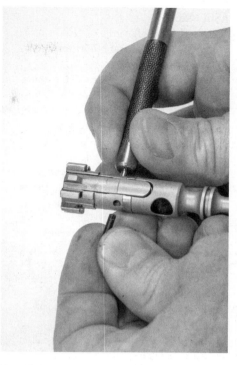

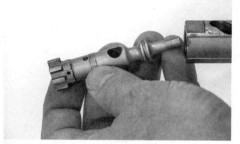

Unless the bolt assembly is very dirty, the bolt should now drop free of the bolt carrier.

You will need a small punch to push out the extractor pin that holds the extractor in place (above). Once the pin is removed, the extractor will separate from the bolt (below).

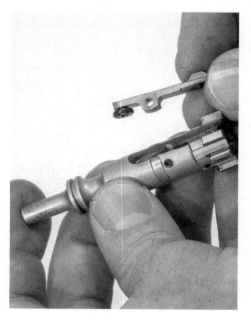

You will need to depress the buffer retainer pin with a pointed object in order to pull the buffer and buffer spring from the buffer tube in the stock.

ASSEMBLY

1. Install the handguards.
2. Install the buffer and buffer spring.
3. Install extractor.
4. Install the bolt into bolt carrier, making sure the extractor is positioned to the right side.
5. Insert the bolt cam pin, so that it is aligned long-ways with the bolt carrier.
6. Insert the firing pin.
7. Insert the firing pin retaining key.
8. Holding the bolt carrier in your hand, the bolt head facing away from you, flip your wrist. This will allow the bolt to slip forward in the bolt carrier and will verify the bolt assembly is together correctly.
9. Install the front action pin, reattaching the upper receiver to the lower receiver.
10. Partially insert the charging handle into the upper receiver.
11. Insert the bolt into the upper receiver and push the bolt and charging handle fully forward.
12. Close the action and push the action pins back in place from right to left.

Now that you know how to take your AR-15 apart and put it back together, so that you may perform each level of maintenance. It is also now time to conduct a function check, to make sure the AR is operational.

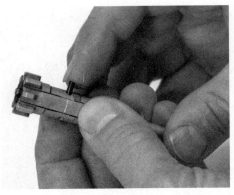

To install the extractor, you will need to insert the extractor retaining pin.

Once inserted, the bolt cam pin will need to be rotated 90 degrees, so that the hole through it is positioned to allow the firing pin to pass through.

The buffer spring and buffer are pushed into the buffer tube and held in place by the buffer retaining pin, which must be depressed to fully seat the buffer.

FUNCTION CHECK

1. Unload and clear.
2. Place the safety selector switch to safe.
3. Depress the bolt lock/release, which will allow the bolt to go forward.
4. Pull the trigger. It should not release the hammer and you should not hear a click.
5. Place the selector switch to the fire position.
6. Pull the trigger and hold it to the rear. The hammer should be released and you should hear a click.
7. While holding the trigger to the rear, pull the charging handle all the way to the rear and release it.

8. Release the trigger and pull it again. The hammer should release and you should hear a click.
9. Insert an empty magazine into the magazine well.
10. Pull on the magazine, to ensure it is locked in place.
11. Pull the charging handle to the rear and release it. The bolt should lock in place.
12. Push the charging handle forward until it locks into place.
13. Depress the magazine release. The magazine should drop free of the AR.

PRE-FIRE INSPECTION

A pre-fire inspection should be performed prior to every day's range session and even periodically, as time permits, throughout a range session. This could be considered similar to a pre-flight inspection performed by a pilot. Once familiar with your AR, this check should not take more than about 60 seconds.

1. Unload and clear.
2. Check that both action pins are fully inserted.
3. Check the pistol grip and stock to ensure they are secure.
4. Check the handguard to see that it is secure.
5. Check your sights and/or scope rings for tightness.
6. Perform a function check.

POST-FIRE INSPECTION

Just as with a pre-fire inspection, perform a post-fire inspection after every range session,

Step 2 of the function check.

Step 4 of the function check.

Step 3 of the function check.

Step 5 of the function check.

as well as throughout a range session as time permits. A post-fire inspection done properly will take about two minutes. You can periodically check various elements of the post-fire inspection individually during breaks in shooting. In other words, you can perform mini post-fire inspections throughout your range session, but always perform a complete post-fire check when the shooting for the day is complete.

1. Unload and clear.
2. Check that both action pins are fully inserted.
3. Check the pistol grip and stock to ensure they are secure.
4. Check the handguard to see that it is secure.
5. Ensure trigger pins are flush with the sides of the lower receiver.
6. Check your sights and/or scope rings for tightness.
7. Remove the bolt to determine how dirty and fouled the parts are.
8. Ensure the bolt will move back and forth inside the bolt carrier, by flipping your wrist.
9. Ensure the carrier key on the top of the bolt is not loose.
10. Install the bolt and perform a function test.

Step 9 of the function check.

Step 12 of the function check (below) and Step 13 of the function check (right).

FIELD-EXPEDIENT CLEANING

A field-expedient cleaning is one performed on the range or the battlefield during breaks in the action. Look at is as washing your hands. Throughout the day, you will wash your hands periodically to remove germs or when they get dirty. Depending on the task at hand, your hands may get very dirty before you wash them, while at other times not so much. You should also perform a field-expedient cleaning as soon as practically possible after you have experienced a stoppage of any type. A post-fire inspection is always a part of a field-expedient cleaning, and it should be performed before and after the cleaning.

1. Unload and clear.
2. Remove the bolt.
3. Disassemble the bolt.

PRE-FIRE CHECKLIST

Check the scope rings and base/bases to ensure they are tight.

Make sure both action pins are fully inserted.

Check the handguard and all attachments to ensure they are secure and in working.

Check the pistol grip and stock to make sure they are secure.

4. Clean and inspect all parts of the bolt.
5. Check the gas rings on the rear of the bolt to ensure they are in place and that the ends of the rings are not aligned in the same spot.
6. Wipe down the internals of the upper receiver.
7. Lube the bolt.
8. Reassemble.
9. Perform a function check.

DETAIL CLEANING

Detail cleanings should be performed after any high-volume fire and before any period of long storage. You should also perform a detail cleaning when your AR has been exposed to lots of moisture, dirt, or dust. A barrel cleaning should, in most cases, be a part of a detailed cleaning, as should a post-fire inspection.

1. Unload and clear.
2. Disassemble the AR.
3. Remove all fouling, dirt, grit, and moisture from all parts.

4. Visually inspect the following parts:
   a. Make sure the hammer and trigger pins are flush with the outside of the lower receiver.
   b. Check that the carrier key is not loose.
   c. Inspect the gas rings.
   d. Inspect extractor.
   e. Check the fit and function of the safety selector switch.
   f. Check that the barrel is tight with the upper receiver.
   g. Check to see that the stock and pistol grip are secure.
   h. Examine the magazine release and bolt lock/release for damage or wear.
   i. Check the tightness of all scope mounts, sights, and accessories.
5. Clean the barrel.
6. Lube as needed.
7. Reassemble.
8. Perform a function check.

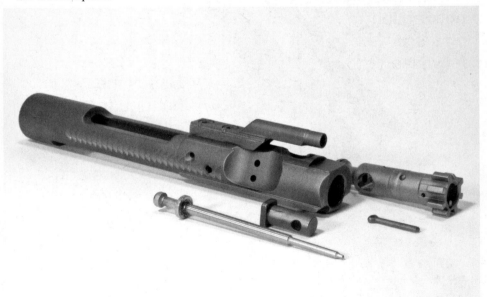

In addition to the steps involved during a pre-fire check, during a post-fire check, you should also inspect the bolt for cleanliness and serviceability.

COMPLETE SERVICE

At a minimum, perform a complete service of your AR once per year, regardless how often it has been fired. During a complete service, you will perform a detailed cleaning, and you will also be looking for problems with your AR such as over-stressed springs and cracked or broken parts.

A complete service of an AR is nothing more than a detailed cleaning with the following additional checks:

1. Check the buffer spring for proper length. For rifles, it should be between 11¾ and 13½ inches long. For carbines, it should be between 10¹/₁₆ and 11¼ inches long. If the spring is outside of these tolerances, replace it.
2. Check all springs for breaks or deformations.

3. Check the torque on the gas key screws on the top of the bolt carrier. They should be between 35 and 40 pounds.

If you are one of those folks who like to do paperwork, you can use the included Bushmaster Rifle Inspection Form and the AR Service Record at the end of this chapter to keep track of and make notes on your cleaning and service activities.

NOTES ON CLEANING AND LUBRICATION

Knowing how to clean and lubricate you AR-15 is just as, if not more, important than knowing when it should be done. Many AR shooters make the mistake of thinking that, since the AR is a mechanical device, it needs to be heavily lubricated. This is not the case. In fact, an AR with too much lube can collect

Anytime you have the bolt separated from the bolt carrier, check the presence, position, and cleanliness of the gas rings on the bolt.

dust, dirt, and grit, causing it to eventually stop running. Of more danger, too much lube, particularly in the area of the barrel and chamber, can create over-pressure situations that can result in damage to the gun and shooter.

There are lots and lots of cleaning products on the market. There are even cleaning kits specifically designed for the AR. You can purchase one of these kits or you can buy the items you need separately. Or, you could do both. Its not a bad idea to have a range or field cleaning kit in conjunction with a more substantial cleaning and tool kit at home, where you are more likely to perform a detailed cleaning or a complete service. Here's a list of all of the tools and cleaning supplies you will need.

1. One-piece, caliber-specific rod to clean the barrel.
2. Caliber-specific wire brushes for cleaning rod.
3. Caliber-specific patch attachment for cleaning rod.
4. Caliber-specific patches for barrel cleaning.

5. Cotton rags.
6. Q-tips or similar cleaning swabs.
7. Cartridge-specific chamber brush.
8. .50-caliber chamber brush.
9. Wire toothbrush.
10. Carbon solvent.
11. Copper solvent.
12. Lubrication.

Now let's look at how to properly use these cleaning tools, so that you get your AR clean and so that you do not damage it in the process. Let's start with the barrel.

A one-piece cleaning rod will protect your barrel. Optionally, you can use a pull-through coated wire rod intended for this purpose. Regardless, always clean a barrel from the chamber end. The goal is to remove as much carbon and copper folding as possible. There are 57 million different ways to clean a barrel and everyone has their own it's-better-than-your method. Here's mine.

I start by running several patches soaked in a carbon solvent down the barrel. I like to use Ballistol. I let the barrel set for about

In order to remove the copper fouling from inside your barrel, you will need patches, a straight or flexible pull-through rod, and a copper solvent.

Bushmaster offers a variety of cleaning and service kits for the AR. Some are suited for the field, while others are complete and better suited for the bench.

30 minutes, and then I run five dry patches down the barrel. Next, I switch to a copper solvent. I like Montana Xtreme Copper Killer. I push five patches coated with Copper Killer down the barrel and wait about 30 minutes. I then follow that up with about five dry patches.

Now, to see if I was successful in removing the copper fouling, I run another patch coated with Copper Killer down the barrel. If it comes out with any blue on the patch, I know there's still copper in the barrel. At this time, you can transition to a more abrasive solvent if you like.

I often use Montana Xtreme Copper Cream. Five coated patches and then five dry patches followed by another single patch coated with Cooper Killer. If the blue is gone, the barrel is free of copper. If not, continue until the single Copper Killer patch comes out white.

The next thing I do is clean the chamber. I do this with an AR chamber brush sized just for the chamber, as well as one that has a large section of bristles on the end to clean the locking lug area. Work this two-stage brush, coated with a carbon solvent, in and out of the chamber for a minute or so, then

You will need a torque wrench to check the bolts on the gas key on top of your bolt carrier. A torque wrench also comes in handy for mounting optics. Weaver manufacturers a scope mounting kit that contains everything you need to mount a scope, including a torque wrench.

Pull-through cleaning rods work very well and are safe to use in your barrel, but they will add time to the process.

Just one company can make a variety of products for cleaning and maintaining the bore of your AR's barrel.

run a few dry patches through the barrel and clean the locking lug area with cotton swabs.

Now I go back to patches soaked in Ballistol and run these down the barrel, alternating with a clean patch until the dry patch comes out white. Now the barrel is free of carbon and copper fouling, and all that's left is to lightly coat the bore with oil. For that, I run one patch soaked with Montana Xtreme's Bore Conditioning Oil down the barrel. I then follow that patch with three to five dry patches. Do *not* leave oil or anything else in the barrel when you are done cleaning it.

Depending on how fouled your barrel is, this process as I've just related it can take anywhere from 15 minutes to two hours or longer. As for the cleaning of the rest of the AR, it is, for the most part, a fairly straight-forward task. Spray Ballistol or any other carbon solvent on the carbon fouled parts, let them soak, and wipe them off. I like to use a .50-caliber bore brush on the side of the bolt carrier and I like to use compressed air, when possible, to blow any debris that might be residing in the nooks inside the upper and lower receivers.

When your AR is clean, you need to lube it, but this does not mean you simply spray the entire gun with WD40 and walk away. There is a method to the madness, and it does not involve a lot of lubrication.

There are as many lubrication options for an AR as there are different flavored suckers in a bag of Dum Dums. I like the Ultima Lube II Grease form Wilson Combat. Is it the best? I have no idea. Experiment with different lubes and choose one you like the best. The key is to put the lubrication in the right place.

1. Put a drop or two of lube on the top of the charging handle. This makes it smooth to operate and eliminates some of the grinding noise you hear when you pull it to the rear.
2. Put some of the grease or lube on your fingers and run them down the buffer spring. This will eliminate some of the noise from the sprig during recoil.
3. With some more lube on your fingers, rub the outer surface of the bolt and the firing pin. Also apply a bit of lube to the gas rings at the end of the bolt.

With a gas impingement-driven AR, the bolt and bolt carrier can become extremely dirty with carbon fouling. You'll need a reliable carbon solvent like Ballistol to clean these parts.

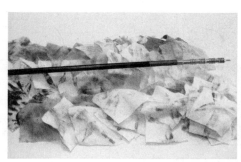

Barrel cleaning can be a chore, consume a lot of patches, and require a lot of effort. All these patches were used to clean one barrel.

If patches soaked in copper solvent are coming out of your bore with any blue color on them (below), you still have copper fouling in your barrel.

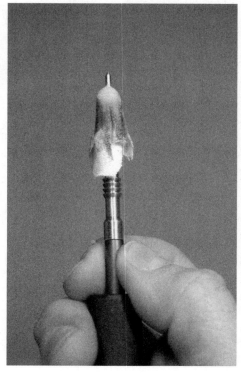

4. With the bolt inserted in to the bolt carrier, apply a drop of lube to the inside of the carrier through the hole where the bolt cam is installed.

5. Finally, apply a drop or two of lube to all the contact surfaces on the exterior of the bolt carrier and to the locking lugs.

That's it. You're done. A three-ounce bottle of lube should last you a long, long time, unless you fight hoards of zombies on a day-to-day basis.

BUSHMASTER RIFLE INSPECTION FORM

BUSHMASTER FIREARMS

Armorer Name: _____

Rifle Serial #: _____

Rifle Model: _____

Date: _____

Component I. FIELD STRIP EXAM	Pass	Fail	Component II. DETAILED EXAM	Pass	Fail
Handguard, grips, stock cracks			Bolt carrier		
Takedown pins tight & don't fall out			Bolt		
Charging handle & bolt move freely			Extractor		
Charging handle locks forward			Ejector		
Ejection port cover locks open/closed			Gas rings		
Bolt moves freely in carrier			Bolt key		
Firing pin does not fall out			Cam pin		
Safety (hammer does not drop)			Gas tube		
Fire (hammer drops)			Barrel & flash suppressor		
Magazine release			Front sight		
Sights adjust as necessary			Rear sight		
Buffer & buffer spring			Forward assist		
Lubrication			Handguard, stock, grip		
Forward assist			Buffer tube		
Bolt catch			Buffer & spring		
Barrel free of debris			Takedown pins		
			Bolt catch		
			Safety selector		
			Hammer		
			Disconnector		
			Trigger		
			Ejection port cover		
			Headspace gage		
			Hammer, Trigger Springs		
			Disconnector spring		
			Lubrication		
			Magazines		
			Optics		
			Slings		
			Lights		
			Carrying case		

Notes:

Inspected By: _____

Test fired on: _____

www.T1G.com

www.Bushmaster.com

AR SERVICE AND CLEANING LOG

AR MANUFACTURER

MODEL

SERIAL NUMBER

ACCESSORIES INSTALLED

DATE	ROUNDS FIRED	CLEANING / SERVICE PERFORMED	NOTES

CHAPTER 11

SHOOTING THE AR–BASICS

The Fundamentals of Marksmanship

As it is with any form of shooting, the key to hitting the target lies in properly aligning the sights and controlling the trigger without disturbing that alignment. In my book *Handgun Training for Personal Protection* (available on www.gundigeststore.com), I called this the "secret." Not so much because it *is* a secret, but because too many instructors put too much emphasis on too many other things. They seem to forget that keeping the sights lined up on the target while you press the trigger is the most important of the marksmanship skills you need to master.

That fact established, there are some other aspects of shooting a rifle that can help keep your "launch pad" solid and consistent and keep the sights on target while you press the trigger. The launch pad is you and your rifle. It is where the bullet is launched from, and, if that platform is unstable, your bullet will not consistently go where you want it to go. This is especially true as the distance to the target increases. So, let's build our shooting platform.

There are multiple facets to making every shot, and you need to be cognizant and practiced in all of them. In fact, you can expect your hit percentage to be reduced

Regardless the position you shoot from or the type of AR you shoot, the basic fundamentals of marksmanship always apply.

by at least 10 percent for each of these points you ignore with each shot you take.

BODY POSITION

The position your body is in when you fire a rifle is critical. There are four basic shooting positions. In order from the most stable to the least they are prone, sitting, kneeling, and standing. Know that the closer your rifle is to the ground, the more stable your launch pad will be. Regardless the position you choose, you need to be comfortable. When you are uncomfortable, your muscles start working, even if only subconsciously, to make you comfortable, and this works against you trying to keep the sights aligned on target. In addition to being comfortable, the following all need be applied.

The butt of the rifle goes on your shoulder. Actually, and particularly because an AR has a perfectly straight stock (i.e., the stock is perfectly in line with the bore of the rifle), you should place the buttstock in the pocket of your shoulder so it has 100-percent contact. With hunting rifles it is, more often than not, desirable for the butt to extend slightly above your shoulder, due to the way those stocks are configured.

Your cheek or, more specifically, your cheekbone, should be resting on the stock. This can be uncomfortable with some of the Mil Spec-style adjustable stocks. For this reason, some companies offer modified versions that have raised or adjustable cheekpieces, as well as other more comfortable, aftermarket stock configurations.

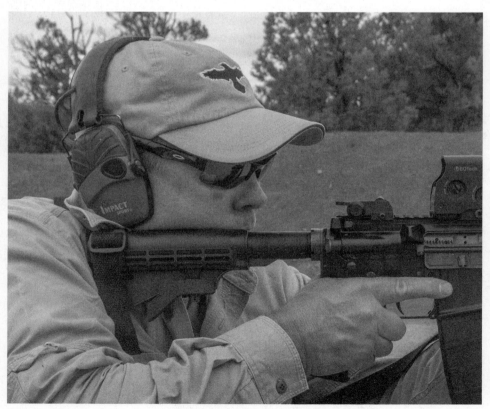

When shooting any rifle, a proper cheek weld is paramount to getting on target swiftly and maintaining control of the rifle.

The prone position is the most stable of all shooting positions, because it is the closest you and your AR can get to the ground.

While your cheekbone is resting on the comb of the rifle, your eye should be looking through the sights. Ideally, you should be able to go to sleep on your AR, wake up, and be looking through the sights without making any adjustment to your head position. If you cannot do this, you are holding the AR incorrectly, the AR's stock does not fit you, or both.

There are two places where your hands grip the stock on an AR. Your shooting hand will wrap around the pistol grip, while your support hand will hold either the handguard or, possibly, a vertical grip attached to a section of rail on your handguard. Some AR shooters like to utilize the magazine well as a vertical fore-grip. Though this is generally a bit too far to the rear to establish a balanced and stable support, it is acceptable. Regardless, you need to understand that you control the rifle with your support hand. Your shooting hand should have a firm but not rigid grip on the pistol grip. If you squeeze the pistol grip too tightly or try to "drive" (move and control) the AR with your shooting hand, it will make trigger manipulation difficult.

Your arms should be under the AR as much as reasonably possible. You do not want your elbows sticking out to the side. This is especially true if you plan to be operating in some sort of tactical situation, where you have to move through tight confines. It's also practical when hunting or while shooting just for fun, because, one way or the other, you have to support the

Your grip with your shooting hand should be firm but not extremely tight. Your support hand is the hand that controls where the rifle is pointed.

rifle—hold it up—and the best way to do this comfortably is with your arms under or as close to under the AR as possible.

Some sport shooters and competitors utilize a fully extended support arm when shooting an AR. This arm position can be useful and does provide a great deal of control if you are engaging in rapid fire. However, if precision accuracy is what you want, a more traditional hold of the AR is preferred.

BREATHING

You have to breath when you shoot, otherwise your body will become starved of oxygen and you will begin to shake. In other words, you do not hold your breath while you are shooting. Instead, you should try

Keep your arms and elbows tucked in close to your body, for added stability and control.

to trigger your shot at your natural respiratory pause (NRP). This is the point in the breathing cycle where you have exhaled and are preparing to inhale, and it is the point in the breathing cycle when you are the most relaxed.

That having been said, when shooting an AR in competition and even for fun, volume fire is very often the norm. You may fire a full magazine of 30 rounds in only a few seconds, and you simply cannot unload all that ambition during your NRP. If you try it, you will end up holding your breath. So,

optic pulls everything together just as if you were playing a video game on a television screen. Still, your eye has to focus on one thing; you cannot just look at everything within the optical field of view and expect to get hits.

With an optical sight, you should concentrate on the exact point of the target where you want your bullet to strike, and you should pull the trigger when your reticle becomes aligned over that spot. If you try to concentrate on the reticle, you will end up "chasing" it, because it is moving—you

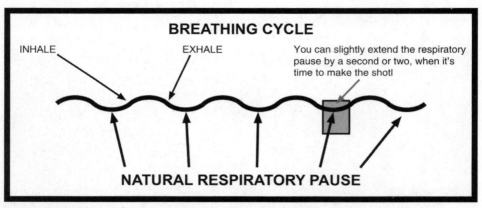

You should try to break your shot during your natural respiratory pause.

when rapidly shooting long strings of fire, try to do it while exhaling, as your body begins to relax. This is, in most cases, not all that hard. If you are in a match or even when shooting recreationally at the range, most high-volume strings of fire are executed at relatively short distances.

SIGHT ALIGNMENT AND SIGHT PICTURE

With optical sights, where your eye can focus on the target and still see the reticle clearly, sight alignment and sight picture are easier to control than they are with open sights. This is because, with optical sights, your eye has to focus only on one plane; the

cannot hold an AR or any firearm perfectly still—and it will become very difficult to break the shot with any consistency.

Open sights are a little different, because there are three planes of focus your eye must deal with: the rear sight, the front sight, and the target. Most AR open sights utilize an aperture rear sight, which nothing but a hole you look through. With just a little practice, your eye will automatically center the front sight in this rear aperture. Sure, it still requires some concentration, but, in the big scheme of sight alignment and sight picture, only about 10 percent of your concentration should be directed to the rear sight.

In addition to the rear component of open sights, you also have concentrate on the target. Regardless the type of shooting you're doing, to properly employ firearms safety rule No. 4 (refer to the sidebar in Chapter 10), which is to always be sure of your target, you must concentrate on the target and, more specifically, the spot on the target you want to hit. Apply about 30 percent of your concentration to the target, the proper spot on the target, and the target surroundings.

You'll focus the remainder of your concentration on the front sight. It should be in clear focus and positioned over the target in the proper place.

NATURAL POINT OF AIM

Always, as much as possible, shoot from your natural point of aim (NPOA). NPOA is very important. NPOA is also misunderstood and often overlooked. In truth, there is no such thing as NPOA, because shooting is not something humans naturally do. It is a *learned exercise*. A better acronym might be CPOA—comfortable point of aim— because what NPOA really means is where your rifle points when you are comfortably in your shooting position. None of this is natural, but the bottom line is it really doesn't matter what we call it, working with it is damned important if you want to hit anything. Here's why.

Understanding proper sight picture and sight alignment when shooting with open sights is critical.

When you get in position, any position, to make a shot, your body should be relaxed and comfortable. If you are relying on muscles to hold the rifle on target, your shakes or the wobble of the sights on the target will be exaggerated and become more so the longer you hold the position.

When you are preparing for a shot, you need to check your NPOA. You do this by briefly closing your eyes and relaxing your head. When you open your eyes, you should still have the proper sight alignment and sight picture. If you do not, you are not shooting with your NPOA, and this means some force you are exerting is influencing your launch platform. Pull the trigger in this instance, and your shot will very likely deviate from your intended point of aim (POA).

Let's say that when you check your NPOA you open your eyes and see that the sights are to the left of the target. The proper

correction is not to push the rifle to the right, rather you should move your entire *body*, your launch platform, to the right. This will allow the rifle to point at the target comfortably. Make sense?

Now, what if you open your eyes to find that you have improper sight alignment? Maybe you can't see a clear and full view through the scope, or maybe the front sight on your rifle has disappeared behind the rear sight. This means your body position is off and the rifle isn't positioned correctly with your body. You should correct your position, recheck your NPOA, and work from there. It could also mean that the sight configuration you have established on your AR doesn't fit your body. You may need that aftermarket stock or an adjustable or bolt-on cheekpiece.

Another version of checking the NPOA can be witnessed when you watch 3-Gun competitors prepare for a stage. They will

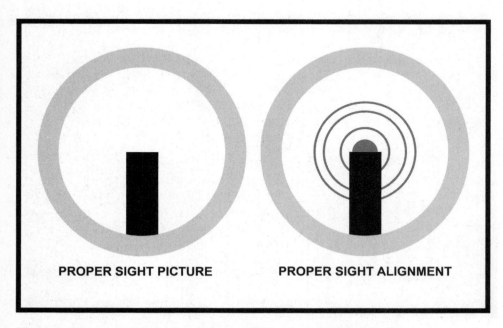

PROPER SIGHT PICTURE   **PROPER SIGHT ALIGNMENT**

When open sights are aligned properly and the proper sight picture is maintained, the front post is centered in the rear aperture and is pointing at the spot on the target you want to hit.

walk through the stage simulating shooting at each of the targets. They do this because speed is of the essence and, during the actual course of fire, they cannot stop and check their natural point of aim. So, what they do is work through the stage in advance to determine their proper body position for engaging each target. Granted, they may have to shoot multiple targets at different angles from the same position, but, by performing this walk-through, they are determining those positions in advance.

I know all this might offer the impression that the preparation for a shot could take several minutes. Well, it might, particularly when you are just beginning to learn all of this. But, as you progress, the process will speed up, and ultimately, hopefully, after several thousand shots, this will all come *naturally.* You will be able to get into position and break an accurate shot within seconds. Doubt me? Consider all the activities constantly involved when driving a car. At first the task seemed insurmountable—check your side mirrors, rear view mirror, seat belt, mirrors again—but now it's all something you do with the same ease as blowing your nose.

Get into a shooting position and close your eyes, relax, and breathe. When you open your eyes, your sights should still be on target. If they are, you are working with your natural point of aim.

TRIGGER CONTROL

If you asked a hundred firearms instructors how to pull a trigger, I'd bet 99 of them will tell you something like this: "Apply constant pressure on the trigger while holding the sights on the target. You should be surprised when the trigger breaks and the rifle fires."

Let me go on record right now as saying this is bullshit. I know, the hate mail will soon be rolling in and my name will be Mudd. However, this is not how you *should* pull a trigger. It is, however, how you should *learn* to pull a trigger.

Here's the thing. Have you ever heard a professional marksman finish a course of fire and say, "Gee, I was surprised every time the gun went off"? Um, I'm guessing the answer is "No." When an experienced person picks up a strange rifle or handgun, they will pull the trigger multiple times before they actually fire. Why? They want to learn the trigger so they can eliminate that surprise when it breaks. They need to know the trigger so they can make it break when they want it to.

Granted, when you are first learning to shoot a firearm, you will be surprised when the trigger breaks. It's just like learning what you can and cannot say around your wife. You can learn this with dry-fire and save a lot of ammo. The same cannot be said of your wife.

Some will point out that the surprise break teaching technique helps to overcome flinching. Well, yeah, after you do it enough. The counterpoint can be offered that the flinch comes from not knowing when the gun will go off, because you are—guess what—expecting a surprise.

Maybe the reason folks stop flinching is because they finally figure out when the trigger will actually break.

That leads me to the next question: When do you break the trigger? Answer: When the sights are aligned on target. If the bang surprises you, you're doing something wrong.

I asked former Marine sniper instructor Caylen Wojcik if he knew when his trigger was going to break or if it was a surprise to him when it did. Caylen said, "I know exactly when it's going to break. If it surprises me, I usually miss." Jacob Bynum, the lead instructor at Rifles Only, agrees with Wojcik. Basically, my contention with the issue is that if you're shooting with the surprise break technique, you're not shooting enough. You have not learned to make the gun go off when you want it to. Ever wonder why shooters get trigger jobs or replace triggers in guns? Well, they do it so they can predict, not guess, when the trigger will break.

So, just how *do* you pull a trigger? You pull a trigger straight to the rear with consistent and uninterrupted rearward pressure. How do you *learn* to pull a trigger? By applying consistent, uninterrupted rearward pressure hundreds if not thousands of times, until you learn when that trigger will break and cause the rifle to fire. You cannot learn it by talking about it and you cannot learn to do anything that will continue to surprise you. You learn how to pull a trigger *by pulling a trigger,* and you pull a trigger smoothly and consistently until it breaks, thus causing the rifle to fire at the precise moment you want it to. That's called trigger control.

FOLLOW-THROUGH

Contrary to trigger control, follow-through, which is what you do immediately after the trigger has released the sear, is a *reaction,* not an action. If your sights are aligned properly, you have the proper sight picture, and if you pulled the trigger without disturbing that sight picture, you will hit the target as long as you follow through properly. If you do not follow through properly, your bullet will not hit the target, and this is regardless how well you do any of those other things.

Trigger control can only be mastered with practice. The good news is that much of this practice can be conducted without firing a single shot.

You properly follow through by doing absolutely nothing other than continuing to execute all the fundamentals of marksmanship. You let the rifle recoil and float back down on target. If your position is correct and if you are using your NPOA, your sights will float back down on target, too, and you can view the results of your shot.

While the rife is in recoil, you should have mentally called your shot. You should have seen the relationship of the reticle or sights on the target, when the trigger broke. In other words you should have a mental impression of where in the wobble the sight or reticle was when you fired the shot. As the target comes back into view—and it will come back into view, if you were exercising your NPOA—you should be able to evaluate the situation immediately. From a hunter's or defensive shooter's standpoint, look at it this way: Once you pull the trigger, it's not over. It's just the beginning. Your new job is to follow through and respond accordingly.

CONCENTRATION

Making a successful shot happens like a surgical procedure. You would not want your brain surgeon distracted with thoughts of his wife cheating on him or wondering how many lobsters he was going to eat for dinner with the money you're paying him, would you? No, of course not. You want your surgeon's complete concentration on the task as hand. That is how you should approach your shooting.

If you are admiring the trophy you are going to win before you have completed the match, you are distracted. If you are eating elk steaks before you shoot your elk, you may go hungry. You need the right mindset to make good shots, and that mindset is to approach each shot with surgical precision. You must fully concentrate on the shot. This is how it's supposed to go, step by step:

1. You see the target.
2. Determine if the shot can safely be taken.
3. Evaluate the situation and determine if you can make the shot.
4. Decide on a position.
5. Get into position.
6. Align the sights.
7. Control your breathing.
8. Check your natural point of aim.
9. Make a final check of the target area for safety.
10. Press the trigger.
11. Follow through and call your shot.
12. Reload if necessary.
13. Assess the situation.
14. Admire your shooting.
15. Post pictures on Facebook and brag to the world.

That's a lot to do for one trigger squeeze, so let's see if we can break it down to a simpler sequence of events.

No matter if you are shooting at close range or at distance, proper follow-through is how you finish the shot.

To start with, you should know your limits. You should know what you can and cannot do with your rifle. If you cannot do it on the range, you cannot do it in the field. You have to have confidence, and the only way to get that is with practice.

Assuming positions should come naturally. So, too, should be your sight alignment and sight picture. You should also not have to think about your sight picture, because you have done all these things in practice. The trigger pull should be natural, and so should the act of following through and calling your shot. As soon as you have evaluated the shot, you should immediately be preparing for follow-up shots.

The shot should be a natural reaction to a situation. It should not be a complicated problem you have to work through. The only way to get to that point is through

With enough practice, you will apply all the basic fundamentals of marksmanship almost subconsciously.

repeated and good practice. When you get into position behind your rifle, there should be a calming sensation that takes over your body, because you have been there before. Before you is a target you know you can hit, because you have hit a target in this situation before.

RANGE ACCESSORIES

To shoot, you need more than just an AR and ammo. You will need targets to shoot and a range on which to shoot them. If you want to improve your shooting and have a way to measure your improvement, you will also need a shot timer. Sandbags are can be very helpful when sighting in a rifle or evaluating ammunition, but what you do not need is a shooting bench; you can zero your rifle and test your ammo from the prone position while using sandbags.

Sandbags can be purchased and then filled on your own. When filled, sand bags should be firm, but they should also offer a little bit of give, so that they can support the AR. You can fill sandbags with the obvious sand, but I've found several things wrong with sand. First, it is heavy, which makes transporting sandbags a pain. It is also susceptible to moisture and can become a mud bag. Finally, if your sandbag develops even a small leak, all the sand can run out in just a few seconds. As a remedy, I've found the little polymer balls used as ammo for airsoft guns to be great sandbag filler. They are light, impervious to moisture, and do not have the tendency to leak out between the threads where a bag is sewn together.

It wasn't all that long ago that shot timers weren't that easy to come across. Only the best shooting shops had them and, when you found one, it cost more than most folks wanted to pay. For the most part, nothing has changed in that realm. However, the advent of the smartphone has made the bulky shot timer in your range bag a thing of the past, at least as far as recreational shooting is concerned. If you have a smartphone, chances are there are several shot timer apps you can download.

What a shot timer gives you is a way to evaluate the speed with which you engage targets. It will measure the total time it took you, and the good shot timers will also tell you the time between each of your shots. For example, let's say you're shooting a drill where you fire one shot from the standing position and the next shot from kneeling. By looking at the shot timer, you can see exactly how long it took you between the first and second shot.

There is no shortage of targets on the market. There are targets for sighting in a rifle, for shooting at long range, for playing games, and for practicing for shooting bad guys, zombies, and animals. You can also make your own targets with markers, crayons, and even the printer to your computer.

To simplify target selection for the shooting drills contained in this book, I have identified a selection of targets from Birchwood Casey for use with each exercise. Birchwood Casey targets were selected for several reasons. For one, they are a one-company resource for every target you need for the drills in this book. Second, the company has been in business a long time and will likely stay in business for a long time, so, if you decide to try these drills 10 years from now, chances are you will still be able to get the targets you need from Birchwood Casey. Finally, I selected Birchwood Casey targets because they are good targets. They work, they are easy to see, and are also readily available most any place that sells shooting stuff.

· **BIRCHWOOD CASEY SHOOT-N-C SELF-ADHESIVE VARIETY PACK**—This collection of self-adhesive circular targets

Sandbags make for a good rest when shooting from the prone position and are advisable when you are zeroing your AR.

A shot timer is a great tool to help you evaluate your shooting ability and speed.

contains two-, three-, and 5½-inch targets, along with one-inch black target pasters, which can be used as targets, too. This is a good collection of targets that can be used for most any of the shooting drills you'll want to attempt with your AR.

· BIRCHWOOD CASEY EZE-SCOREER

TQ-19—This is a large paper target used by many law enforcement agencies for training and qualification. It simulates a human torso and can be used in conjunction with any of the circular Shoot-N-C targets from the Variety Pack.

· BIRCHWOOD CASEY SHOOT-N-C CORRUGATED SILHOUETTE DIE CUT

KIT—This is another great defensive training target and one that is also weather resistant. Additionally, it's a great target to use if you're setting up a range where you do not have rigid target stands at the distances you need. This target can be used in conjunction with the self-adhesive Variety Pack.

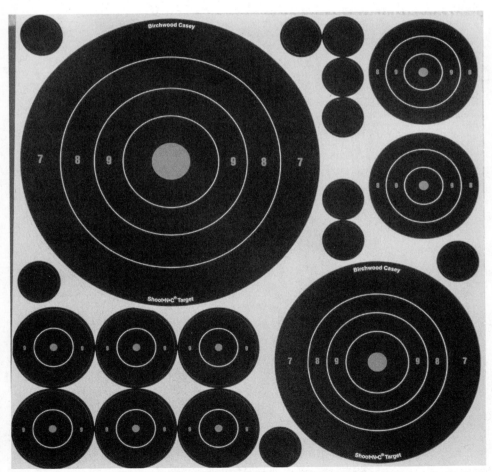

The Birchwood Casey Shoot-N-C Self Adhesive Variety Pack contains a variety of targets that can be shot by themselves, or they can be pasted to other, larger targets, if desired.

- **BIRCHWOOD CASEY PRE-GAME COYOTE AND DEER**—Hunters understand the importance of shot placement, and shooting at a target that replicates the animal you intend to hunt helps you be better prepared to make the shot. Cops shoot at targets that look like bad guys, soldiers shoot at targets that look like the enemy, and bowhunters shoot at targets that look like the animals they will be hunting. Why should someone who hunts with an AR practice any differently?

- **BIRCHWOOD CASEY STICK-A-BULL SIGHT-IN**—When sighting in your AR, it's nice to have a target with a one-inch grid, to help you determine how much adjustment you need to make. This self-adhesive target can be placed at whatever distance you need to sight in, and it can also be used in conjunction with the Variety Pack if you need a larger, easier to see center aiming point.

- **DARKOTIC SAMPLE PACK**—Sometimes we just shoot for fun. Zombie targets, pop cans, old fruit, or any other safe target only makes recreational shooting more enjoyable. The more fun you have while shooting, the more you'll shoot, and the more you shoot, the better marksman you'll become.

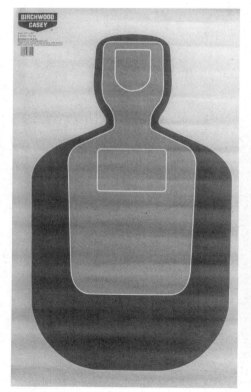

Birchwood Casey's Eze-Scoreer TQ-19 target is one used by many law enforcement agencies for training and qualification. You can enhance it by sticking other self-adhesive Birchwood Casey targets to it.

Shoot-N-C Corrugated Silhouette Die Cut Kit (below) and the Stick-A-Bull Sight-In target (right).

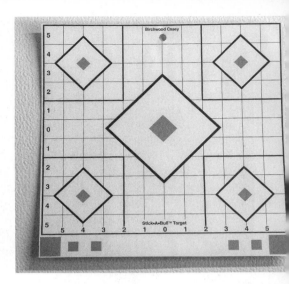

Sometimes shooting is done just for fun, and cool targets like the Birchwood Casey Darkotic Sample Pack can be a blast to blast.

Lifelike animal targets are smart for hunters to practice on.

STEEL TARGETS

Steel targets are fun to shoot at, because you get immediate visual and audible feedback. Not only are they fun, this instant feedback aids in training, too.

The problem with most steel targets is that they are heavy and expensive, and both these things make them not very well suited to the recreational shooter. Thankfully, Wyatt Tubb, of Tubb Enterprises, in Texas (210-296-6784; tubbenterprises@gmail.com), has come up with an affordable and lightweight steel target system that's easily transportable and can be set up just about anywhere.

The targets come with a stake and a stake driver. The really great thing about this system is that you can drive this stake into the ground anywhere, from a flat surface to the side of the steepest mountain. Essentially, with the Tubb Stake Target, you can make a rifle range anywhere. Several configurations are available. Cost-wise, they are less than 500 rounds of ammo, yet should last a lifetime.

CHAPTER 12

ZEROING THE AR

Back before cell phones and before everyone had Internet access, zeroing or sighting in your AR was simple. I'm not saying cell phones or the Internet have made it complicated, but, back in the pre-wired-in era, the sights on ARs were fairly standard. That's not the case anymore, of course, but, from a practical standpoint, zeroing an AR is no different now than zeroing any other rifle.

Your AR should be zeroed at a distance that fits with how it's intended to be used. Just because a gun writer, the military, or some tactical guy on TV stipulates a 300-yard zero means you have to follow suit. What if you're only going to shoot at 100 yards? Indeed, since the AR is a derivative of the M16, which was intended as a combat weapon, many think that ARs have to have some sort of military inspired, "combat type" zero. That's not the case. Zero your AR so that it will best allow you to shoot at and hit the things *you* intend to shoot at with it.

Depending on the ammunition, your trajectory can vary a great deal, showing extreme variations in point of impact (POI) in relation to point of aim (POA). If you plan on employing an AR as a battle rifle,

If you plan to hit what you shoot at, establishing a proper zero with your AR is critical.

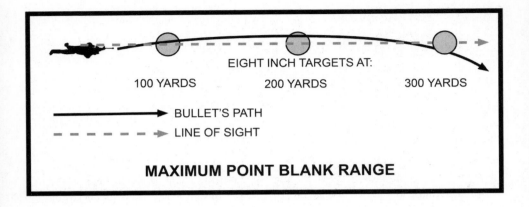

EIGHT INCH TARGETS AT:

100 YARDS   200 YARDS   300 YARDS

→ BULLET'S PATH

- - → LINE OF SIGHT

MAXIMUM POINT BLANK RANGE

the maximum point blank range (MPBR) method has merit.

The MPBR premise is being able to hold dead center on your target over the longest distance possible and still get effective hits. MPBR depends primarily on two things: target size and trajectory. For example, the Black Hills 69-grain Sierra MatchKing load will produce about 2,700 fps from an AR-15 with a 16-inch barrel. If you specify an

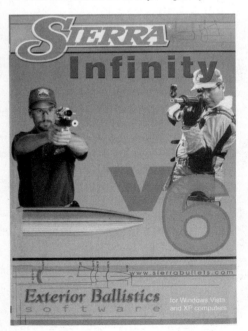

eight-inch target, the Sierra Infinity ballistics program will indicate that the MPBR for that load, at that velocity, is 296 yards. This means the bullet should not rise above or fall below the line of sight (LOS) more than four inches from the muzzle all the way out to 296 yards. In other words, if you hold dead center on an eight-inch target, your bullet should hit that eight-inch target anywhere between the muzzle and 296 yards away.

Switch to the Hornady 40-grain V-Max with a velocity of about 3,350 fps and the MPBR with an eight-inch target changes to 330 yards. What's interesting is that to achieve a MPBR zero for the 69-grain load, you can zero at 33 yards. For the 40-grain V-Max, you'd need to zero at 39 yards. Experience has shown that sighting-in the open sights on an AR somewhere between 30 and 40 yards will generally produce an MPBR for an eight-inch target with most .223 Remington loads.

There is one concern. The problem with an eight-inch target MPBR zero is that your rifle will be shooting about three inches high at 100 yards. If that's okay with you

A ballistics program like the Sierra Infinity is a great tool to help you understand your bullet's trajectory and to help you make decisions regarding your proper zero.

Before establishing the zero on your AR, consider all the variables.

and you can hold to make the correction when trying to make a precision shot when shooting at 100 yards, no worries. If you want your 100-yard POA/POI to be the same, then zero at 100 yards. Just remember, if you zero at 100 yards, you'll be about a foot or more low at 300 (depending on your ammunition, of course).

AR carbines are often employed at very close range and, if you're keeping one for home-defense, you need to be able to deliver accurate fire up close. Because the open sights are about 2½ inches above the bore, your bullet will strike about that far below your POA inside 10 yards. If you are trying to shoot a zombie in the head across your living room, this could get tricky.

To fully grasp the sighting-in process, you need to understand the flight of the bullet. As soon as the bullet exits the barrel, gravity begins to take affect. The pull of gravity is a constant, which means that no matter which

SIGHT OFF-SET AT CLOSE RANGE

bullets you fire from your AR, if the barrel is parallel to the ground, it will take all of those bullets the same amount of time to drop to the ground. In real life, since some bullets are going faster than others, they will travel a further distance from the muzzle before they strike the ground.

We compensate for this immediate drop in trajectory by adjusting our open sights or our optical sight so that, when we look through them, our line of sight intersects with or crosses the bullet's path. In most instances, our line of sight will cross the bullet's path at both a very close distance and at a much further distance. The important thing for you to do is to decide at which distance you want your line of sight to cross the bullet's path. This all depends on the type of shooting you intend to do with your AR.

Let's say you want to hunt prairie dogs with your AR and you have fitted it with a rifle scope that has a bullet drop compensating reticle. Depending on the brand of scope and the reticle style, it will probably specify a 100- or 200-yard zero. This will allow the additional aiming points on the reticle to coincide to designated ranges beyond 100 or 200 yards. While you're shooting prairie dogs, all you'll need to do is hold the aiming point appropriate to the distance to the little prairie rat and squeeze the trigger. This system works just fine and, in fact, could be employed for other types of shooting, be it big-game hunting or competition.

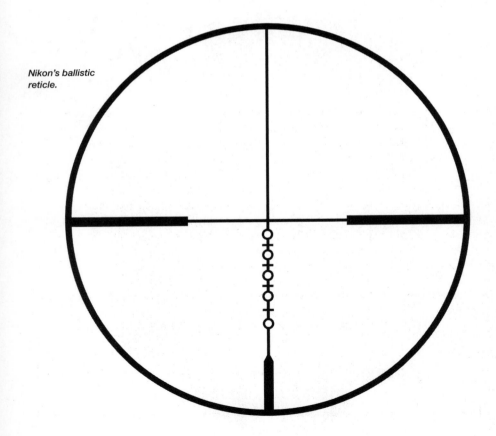

Nikon's ballistic reticle.

On the other hand, you might be using an optic that has target turrets. With these, your intention is to dial in the correct vertical adjustment, based on the range to the target, with the elevation adjustment turret. If this is your plan, then you'll want to sight your AR in at 100 yards and then, with the help of a ballistics program and time on the range, confirm exactly how many clicks you need to dial in at further distances.

The previously mentioned MPBR is another option for zeroing, but it is best applied when your target is not very small. If you are shooting zombies out to 300 yards and need to put the bullet in their heads, it may not be the best solution. On the other hand, if your goal is to shoot a terrorist in the torso, zeroing with the MPBR concept based on an eight- or even 12-inch target should work just fine. The military and most tacticians suggest a 300-yard zero with the small aperture of conventional sights. With most loads, a 25-yard zero will get you close to a 300-yard zero, because the bullet will cross the LOS at 25 yards and again at about 300 yards. Of course, this can all vary, based on how high your open sights are or your optical sight is above the bore of your AR.

Regardless the zeroing method you use, here are some tips to help you through the actual process of zeroing open sights.

First, set the sights to mechanical zero. For the front sight this means turning it until the base of the post is level with the

Target turrets.

Before zeroing open sights, adjust the front sight to mechanical zero so that the base of the front post is flush with the base of the sight window.

Before zeroing open sights, adjust the aperture in the rear sight to its mechanical zero, so that it is in the middle of the sight housing.

On A2-style sights with an elevation dial, set the dial to either the 6/3 or 8/3 position, before you begin the zeroing process.

sight housing. For the rear sight, move the windage adjustment knob until the aperture is in the center of the housing. If the rear sight is of the A2 style, set the dial to either the 6/3 or 8/3 position.

Second, fire a three-shot group at a close target, generally something between 25 and 40 yards, depending on the zero you desire. If you are trying to establish a 100-yard zero, your POI should be about 1½ inches below your POA at 25 yards. If you are going for the MPBR zero, strive to adjust your POI to match your POA at about 30 to 35 yards. If you have a rear sight adjustable for windage and elevation, you can use it to move your POI to match your POA. If you have a rear sight with a range indicator, like the A2-style sight, adjust elevation with the front sight and windage with the rear sight.

When making sight adjustments, remember you move the rear sight the direction you want the bullet to move to match your POA. When adjusting the front sight, the opposite applies. For example, if the bullet impacts low left in relation to your POA, you would move the rear sight to the right and the front sight down.

The click value for the sights will vary with barrel length and sight design. Generally, you can expect each windage click to

These AR shooters are establishing the zero for and sighting in their rifles. They are in the prone position and using sandbags for a rest.

move the POI between 0.5- and 0.75-minute of angle (MOA). Each click of the front sight will move the POI between 1.5 and 2.0 MOA. For all practical purposes, a single MOA equals one inch at 100 yards (or about a ¼-inch at 25 yards).

Once zeroed at close range, confirm and adjust at the longer zero range. If you're using the MPBR zero, you'll need a ballistics program to give you the exact range where the bullet will once again cross your line of sight. Alternately, you can guess. With an eight-inch target as a basis for your MPBR, your long-range zero will be close to 250 yards, depending on the ammo used. The most important thing when zeroing the iron sights on your AR is that you establish a zero you can work with, one that will complement the type of shooting you intend to do.

But what about traditional rifle scopes and other optical sights? The process is very similar, but, in some instances, your optical sight might be higher above the bore than your open sights. With a traditional rifle scope, when you adjust the vertical or horizontal turrets, you are moving the reticle within the scope. Scope adjustments are marked to tell you which way to turn the dial to achieve the desired affect.

With most rifle scopes, you'll twist the vertical adjustment counterclockwise to

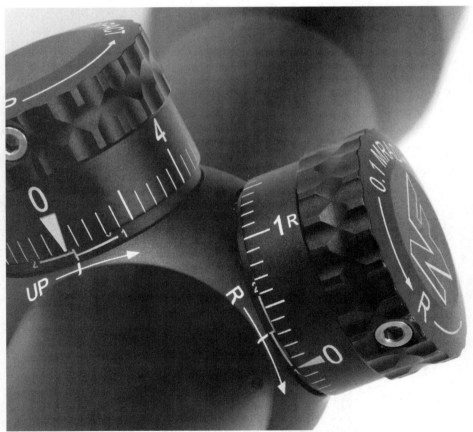

With most optical sights, you will turn the reticle adjustment turrets counterclockwise to move the reticle up or to the right.

move the bullet impact in the up direction on the target. You will also twist the horizontal adjustment counterclockwise to adjust the bullet's point of impact to the right on the target. In most cases, each click on the adjustment dial will equal ¼-MOA or ¹/₁₀-Mil at 100 yards. These readjustments are angular so that, at 200 yards, each click would equal ²/₄- or ½-MOA, or ²/₁₀-Mil.

Mils, MOAs, and inches can be confusing, so some explanation is in order. This is a confusing subject, because humans relate things to known standards. We cannot measure stuff without reference to something we know and understand, such as inches. You'll ask your buddy, "How big was that smallmouth bass?" he'll say, "Oh, about 19 inches," and you'll know exactly how big that fish was, no matter how far his arms are stretched apart. When it comes to shooting, however, it's not all about inches.

There are, essentially, three different ways to correct for trajectory or windage: Mil, MOA, and the inch. The inch method is most generally employed by something called "Kentucky windage," or holding off target with your sights, to compensate for wind deflection and/or bullet drop. It's not really a WAG (wild-ass guess), but more of a SWAG (scientific wild-ass guess).

Mil and MOA differ from an inch because they are an angular, not a linear, measurement. An inch equals an inch no matter how far away it is. A Mil or an MOA represents a different linear measurement that's dependent on the range at which you're looking. With the MOA and Mil systems, you correct the position of the reticle inside the scope based on the wind deflection and trajectory of the bullet at the target's range. Which system is best? It depends as much on the situation as on the shooter, but here's how they work.

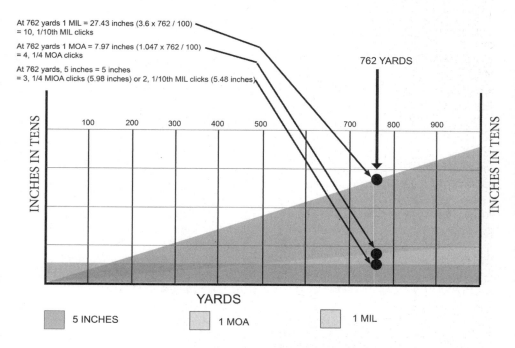

This diagram shows how both MOA and Mil measurements are angular and how they each compare at different distances.

INCHES

This is easy. An inch is one-twelfth of a foot. If something measures 36 inches at 1,000 yards (that's one Mil, but more on that later), guess what? When it's at 753 yards, it's *still* 36 inches long. So, if a bullet drops 36 inches at 500 yards, just hold three feet, the same as a yard, high for your next shot.

MOA METHOD

MOA stands for "minute of angle." There are 360 degrees in a circle, and each degree is divided into 60 minutes. If we round to the nearest one-one hundredth of an inch, at 100 yards a degree measures 62.83 inches. One-sixtieth of that (one MOA) measures 1.047 inches. It's imperative you understand that MOA is proportional to distance. One MOA at 100 yards equals 1.047 inches; at 200 yards it equals 2.094 inches (2 x 1.047). To calculate an MOA at any distance, multiply 1.047 by the distance in yards and divide that number by 100.

On rifles copes with ¼-MOA adjustments, each click equals .261 inches at 100 yards. There's another MOA known as "shooter's MOA" (SMOA). SMOA is nothing but the conversion of a true MOA (1.047 inches at 100 yards) rounded to one inch at 100 yards. SMOA is easier to calculate, because you drop the fraction of an inch. Most scopes have true ¼-MOA click adjustments, but some have ¼-SMOA click adjustments. Does it matter? Well, the difference in an MOA and an SMOA is .047-inch at 100 yards, and nearly a half-inch, 0.47-inch, at 1,000 yards, right? Precisely yes, practically no.

THE MIL METHOD

Mil (milliradian) is another angular measurement. There are 6.2832 (pi x 2) radians per circle. There are 1,000 Mils per radian, so there are 6,283.2 Mils in a circle. There are 21,600 MOA in a circle and 3.4377 MOA per Mil. At 100 yards, 3.4377 MOA equals 3.599 inches (3.4377 x 1.047).

So, rounded up, one Mil equals 3.6 inches at 100 yards.

A Mil is so large we need to break it into tenths, in order to make precise adjustments. If you have a rifle scope with Mil adjustments, each click equals $^1/_{10}$-Mil. This means one-tenth of a Mil equals .36-inch (or .9144-centimeter) at 100 yards. Now, hang with me a bit longer. Since one-tenth of a Mil is an angular measurement, it will be slightly larger at 100 meters than at 100 yards, because 100 meters equals 109.361 yards. At 100 meters, one-tenth of a Mil equals .9999 centimeters. Practically speaking, one-tenth of a Mil equals one centimeter at 100 meters.

As it is with an MOA, a Mil is proportional to distance. One Mil at 100 yards equals 3.6 inches, it's 7.2 inches at 200 yards, and so on. To calculate how many inches are in a Mil at any distance, multiply 3.6 times the distance in yards and divide by 100.

PRACTICAL APPLICATION

This is all really one big math problem that makes my head hurt. I don't think shooting should require a calculator or a bottle of Excedrin. According to former Marine sniper Caylen Wojick, working with Magpul Dynamics, "It's safe to say that the era of MOA scopes (in a tactical application) is over and the new era of Mil scopes is here to stay." Modern Marine snipers work with the Mil method every day—and they don't think in inches, they think in Mils. If you learn the Mil system and work with it frequently, it has advantages. For instance, it works perfectly with a Mil-Dot reticle and it takes fewer clicks than the MOA method to make the same correction.

The MOA system might be more user-friendly for the average shooter, because an MOA is comparable to an inch, at least at 100 yards. Where it requires practice and math is when you're trying to make a

This rifle scope has ¼-MOA adjustments. That means each click of the target turret will move the reticle ¼-inch at 100 yards or one full inch at 400 yards.

correction at say, 523 yards or some other range that does not end in two zeros. Then you'll need to know what each ¼-MOA click equals at that range. You do this by multiplying .26 (¼-MOA) by the distance to the target in yards and then dividing that number by 100. In the case of 523 yards, a single ¼-MOA click would equal 1.35 inches. I find this painful to talk or even write about.

Regardless which type adjustments your optic has, they all take practice to be applied efficiently in the field. So, let's assume you want to sight your AR's optical sight in at 100 yards. What's the process? Start by placing a Birchwood Casey Sight-In target at 25 yards. Now, get into the prone position behind some sandbags. You'll want to fire a three-shot group, aiming at the center of the target. Once that's done, go downrange and mark the center of that three-shot group, then measure the distance from the group center to a point below the center of the target that should allow your POA to match your POI at 100 yards. In most cases you will want your bullet to strike about 1½ inches low at 25 yards for your POA and POI to match at 100 yards.

For the sake of this illustration, let's assume your group is 1.8 inches left and 3.6 inches below a spot that is 1.5 inches below the center of the target. Now, let's assume your optical sight has click adjustments that equal ¼-MOA. At 25 yards, each click will equal one-fourth of ¼-MOA, because 25 yards is one-fourth of 100 yards. That means each click will equal $\frac{1}{16}$-inch at 25 yards. To make the 1.8 inch *right* adjustment, you will need to dial in 28 clicks, which should move the reticle 1.75 inches at

When you are sighting in your AR, if you intend to shoot with a suppressor, then make sure you zero your AR with the suppressor installed.

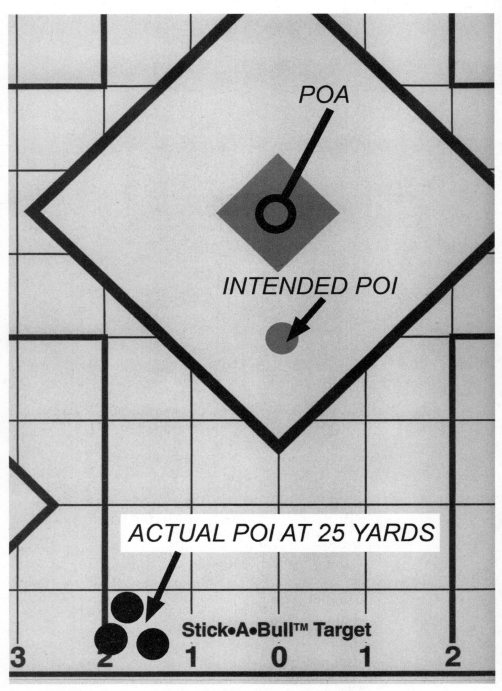

POA

INTENDED POI

ACTUAL POI AT 25 YARDS

Stick•A•Bull™ Target

3   2   1   0   1   2

The proper correction in clicks for an MOA- or a Mil-adjustment scope at 25 yards for this target would be: MOA = 28 clicks right, 58 clicks up; Mil = 21 clicks right, 43 clicks up. Each grid line on the target represents one inch.

This is the kind of group you hope to shoot at 100 yards with your AR. Now all you need to do is to make an adjustment to put this group in the center of the target. This group is about 2.5 inches right and about 0.75-inch high. What's the correct adjustment in MOA? In Mils? You can find the answer at the end of this chapter.

25 yards. You'll also need one click for every $^1/_{16}$-inch you need to move the reticle in the *up* direction, in this example, 58 clicks.

With those adjustments made, fire another three-shot group from 25 yards, find the group center, and make any final adjustments. Now you need to move the target out to 100 yards and fire another three- to five-shot group. You'll need to find the center of that group and make your final adjustments to move the POI to the POA at 100 yards. At this distance, each ¼-MOA click will only move the reticle ¼-inch.

Let's consider the same situation, but now you're using a scope that has $^1/_{10}$-Mil adjustments, so you'll need to convert this measurement to Mils, in order to know how much correction to make.

At 25 yards, each click on a scope with $^1/_{10}$-Mil adjustments will move the reticle about one-twelfth of an inch, so just multiply 1.8 by 12 and you'll see that, to make a 1.8-inch correction, you'll need to dial in 21 to 22 clicks. For the 3.6-inch adjustment, you'll need 43 clicks (3.6 x 12 = 43.2). Once confirmed at 25 yards, move to a 100-yard target and make your final adjustments. Just remember, at 100 yards, each click on the scope with $^1/_{10}$-Mil adjustments will equal $^1/_{10}$-Mil, or .36-inch.

TABLE 1: INCH / MOA / MIL COMPARISON					
RANGE	**1 INCH**	**1 MOA**	**1/4 MOA**	**1 MIL**	**1/10 MIL**
		(4 clicks)	(1 click)	(10 clicks)	(1 click)
(yards)	(inch)	(inches)	(inches)	(inches)	(inches)
100	1	1.04	0.26	3.60	.36
200	1	2.08	0.52	7.20	.72
300	1	3.14	0.78	10.8	1.08
400	1	4.16	1.04	14.4	1.44
500	1	5.20	1.30	18.0	1.80
600	1	6.24	1.56	21.6	2.16
700	1	7.28	1.82	25.2	2.52
800	1	8.32	2.08	28.8	2.88
900	1	9.36	2.34	32.4	3.24
1000	1	10.4	2.60	36.0	3.60

The correct adjustment to move the POI to the center of the target in the image on page 171 is: MOA = left 10 clicks, down three clicks; Mil = left seven clicks, down two clicks.

CHAPTER 13

SHOOTING POSITIONS

You learn to shoot a rifle just like you learn to walk, from the ground up. The further away your rifle gets from earth, the harder it is to shoot accurately.

There are four basic shooting positions, and these can be employed either supported or unsupported. A supported position is one where you are using a stable object, such as a sandbag, stump, tree limb, or shooting sticks, to help you support the rifle. An unsupported position is where you are supporting the rifle with nothing but your body parts.

If you are just learning to shoot an AR or if you are just beginning to learn the shooting positions, you should start in the lowest position possible, and you should also start with a support. It is easier to learn each position if you start in the supported version, because you will be more stable and, in turn, get a better idea of your capabilities.

Many things can be used as a support during shooting, such as a hunting pack, logs, trees, and shooting sticks. A supported position is always preferred over an unsupported position, because it is more stable. Your ability to recognize various supports and to work with them from various positions will allow you to be more successful, say, when hunting or in a defensive situation. You want to evaluate the situation and react quickly. You do not want to stand around expecting a shooting bench to magically materialize while you're in a gunfight.

Unsupported positions could be considered "hasty positions," positions you must assume at a moment's notice. These moments can occur during hunting or in a defensive situation. You may also be required to shoot from an unsupported position in competition. It is always better to shoot from support of some kind, but, support of some kind is not always available.

PRONE

The supported prone position is the most stable of all shooting positions. Your rifle is close to the ground, most of your body is in contact with the ground, and the wind cannot blow you around. If you plan to reach out to the limits of your maximum practical range, this is the position you should choose.

To get into the supported prone position, you will need a rest for your AR like a sandbag or a bipod. In the prone position, your body should be almost perfectly in line with the barrel, but comfort is also important, so a little deviation from this alignment is permissible. Your legs should be spread at a comfortable angle. This is similar to the prone position all those little green plastic army men you used to play with came in. If you are shooting beyond 300 yards, especially at small targets, make sure you get straight behind the rifle. This will make your NPOA easier to obtain, and it will help you control the recoil better.

Your feet should be turned out; do not dig your toes into the ground. Your legs and feet should also be relaxed. Do not try to muscle the rifle onto target by moving your legs or by trying to apply pressure this way

In the prone supported position, you can use your support arm to support the rear of the AR at the stock, or you can also use it to hold onto the handguard.

From the prone unsupported position, both elbows are on the ground and tucked tight against your body and under the AR as much as possible.

or that with your legs or arms. Relax. Place your AR over the support. The AR should rest on the sandbags at a point just forward of the magazine. Of course, an overly long magazine can hamper the prone position, so be cognizant of your equipment and how it will interact with such a position before you begin your practice session or go afield.

Both elbows should be on the ground and the rifle should be tight into your shoulder pocket. Obviously, your shooting hand is placed at the grip of the rifle, but you have two options regarding where to put your support hand; you can place it under the forearm directly above the rest, or you can place it under the toe of the stock, sort of resting the bottom of the stock in the valley between your thumb and index finger. It can sometimes be helpful to have your support hand under the forearm of the rifle. It gives you some added control over the rifle and

allows you to have better and more immediate control over the rifle should you have to switch positions in a hurry.

With the prone unsupported position, the rifle is being supported with nothing but your arms. Nothing changes with your shooting arm; your shooting hand still has control of the AR's grip and your shooting elbow is still on the ground. However, with your support arm, you will have to grasp the AR either along the handguard or you may use the magazine well as a forward vertical grip. Your shooting elbow rests on the ground.

SITTING

There are a number of ways to sit behind a rifle. You can sit with your legs spread wide and your elbows resting on your knees, or you can set cross-legged with your ankles tucked under your legs and your elbows resting on your shins. Your flexibility will

It's important to know how to get into the prone position. Start standing in the outdoor ready position (top left). Drop to the double kneeling position (top right). Fall forward and catch yourself with your support hand (above) and then fully assume the prone position (below). These steps work equally, whether assuming the prone supported or unsupported positions.

determine how low you can go either way. So, too, will the angle to the target and the grass, foliage, or other barriers between you and the target. In high grass, you may have to sit open-legged, with your elbows on your knees in order to get the rifle above any obstructions.

The primary rule of all shooting positions still applies: the closer your rifle to the ground, the more accurate you will be. In either case, your shoulders should be at about a 70- to 80-degree angle in relation to the target. For a field support, you may be using a log, rock, or tree limb. For practice, you'll probably be using shooting sticks.

The more vertical you can make your forearms, the more support you will have. In other words, try to keep your arms as close as you can to the rifle; don't be sticking your elbows out to the side. Your support hand can be tucked into your body and on the toe of the buttstock, just like when shooting in the prone supported position. However, when using two-legged shooting sticks, it's generally better to hold onto the sticks with your support hand.

Many shooters like to use a sling to help support their rifle, when shooting from the unsupported seated position. By tightly looping the sling over either your shooting

The sitting supported position is a very stable position and can often be applied effectively in many shooting situations.

arm or support arm elbow, you can impart some tension into the position. However, never use a tight sling when shooting, unless it is attached to a free-floating handguard. Otherwise, you will induce stress into the launch platform, which will negatively affect your point of impact. In fact, you can use the sling from any position, if it makes you more stable. Just as it is when shooting from the prone position, you must use both arms to support the rifle, and your ability to get close to the ground will depend on your flexibility and intervening obstacles.

KNEELING

The kneeling supported position is only moderately more stable than standing, but, if you can kneel and sit back on your ankle, stability increases a great deal. The most common mistake made with this position is kneeling on the wrong knee. With a forward support, you should kneel on your support-side knee. This allows you to rest your shooting elbow on your shooting side knee.

The goal with the kneeling position, if at all possible, is to keep your lower leg at a 90-degree angle to the earth. This allows

A sling can help steady almost any position, but to use one properly and quickly, you will need to practice. Here's a tip: it needs to be tight.

You can shoot from the seated position with your legs spread, but it's more stable if you tuck your ankles under your legs. This also allows you to get lower, and lower is always more stable.

By tightly looping the sling over your shooting or support elbow, you can add some rigidity to the launch platform.

for the maximum in support, when you need to rest your shooting elbow on your knee. You can pretty much assume that for every degree your leg is off plumb with the ground, your shot will be off a comparable degree. Rest your shooting elbow on your knee and place your support hand either under the toe of the stock, under the fore-arm, or use it to hold the shooting sticks.

When shooting from the unsupported kneeling position, you should kneel on your shooting-side knee and your support arm elbow should rest on your support-side knee. As it is with the seated position, you can also use a sling to help steady the launch platform.

When shooting from the kneeling position and utilizing a support, your support-side knee should be on the ground and your shooting elbow should be rested on your shooting-side knee.

The unsupported kneeling position isn't much more stable than the standing unsupported position, but it does allow you to get closer to the ground. When shooting unsupported from the kneeling position, rest your support elbow on your support knee or rise up if you need to, in order to shoot over some obstruction between you and your target.

DOUBLE-KNEE KNEELING

There is another kneeling position where you simply drop to both knees. It is very fast to assume, but provides less stability. However, and again, depending on your knees, flexibility, and intervening obstacles, it may be your only option. With the double-knee kneeling position, you shoot just the same as you would if you were standing.

CROUCHED

Rumor has it this position came about during combat in Vietnam, where soldiers needed to get low behind a dike, while negotiating rice paddies. It provides a shooting position as stable as the unsupported kneeling position, but it does not allow you to adjust your elevation as much. You are either all the way down or all the way up,

Kneeling positions are fast to assume, and the double-kneeling position might be the fastest. You simply drop to both knees.

there is no in between. It is also hard on your knees, and many shooters simply find it to difficult to maintain the position and recover from it.

STANDING SUPPORTED

Generally, this is done when shooting off of sticks or when resting over a limb or maybe even a vehicle. Your body—your shoulders—should be at about a 90-degree angle to the rifle. You don't want to shoot across your body, like you might have seen in competitive rifle shooters, where they assume a standing position bladed to the target. Rather, you want your body to control and absorb the recoil, and this is best done if you are squared up to the rifle.

Your feet should be shoulder width apart and your legs should be straight (though only if your supporting object is strong enough to support your body weight, such as would be a vehicle hood). If your legs are bent, then you're using muscle, not bone, to maintain your position, and muscles, of course, are not as strong or as rigid as bone. With a flimsy forward support, you will need to slightly bend your legs to help you control recoil.

If you have good knees and need an intermediate position that is quick to assume, the crouched position works very well.

Keep the elbow of your shooting arm low; do not poke it out to the side. Also, do not try to pull the rifle into your shoulder with your shooting hand. Gently hold the grip of the rifle. If you try to pull on the stock with your shooting hand, it will become very difficult to manipulate the trigger with any efficiency.

As for your support hand, it's generally best to keep it under the rifle and slightly forward of the magazine, though some shooters like to use the magazine well as a vertical front fore-grip. If you are shooting off of a log or tree limb, your support hand can go between the rifle and the support. If you are shooting off of a self-supporting rest (one that will stand on its own), you can do the same. This also allows you to keep total control of the rifle during recoil and follow through, plus you may you have to switch positions quickly, and this position accommodates that.

When shooting from the standing unsupported position, you still want your shoulders to be perpendicular to the rifle. Your feet should be about shoulder width apart, your knees should be bent a bit and over your toes. Your shoulders should be

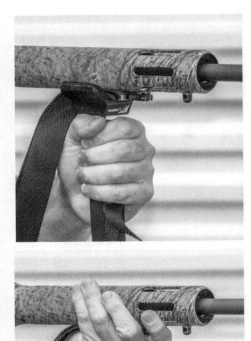

When shooting from the standing supported position, you can apply techniques, such as using the sling, used in any other position (left). You can hold onto your support with your support hand (top right), or you can grasp the handguard with your support hand and then rest your hand on the support (bottom right).

over your knees. This gives you a slight weight-forward stance, which will help you better control recoil.

UNCONVENTIONAL POSITIONS

One thing you can be sure of is that, whether hunting, competing, or in tactical situations, things often don't go as planned and you may be tasked with shooting from some unconventional position.

Adapt and overcome, as they say. Be ready for anything. If you practice from all

While the standing unsupported position might be the most common position from which to shoot an AR, it is the least stable. Only use it if no other option exists.

the positions mentioned, you will be better prepared to handle what reality throws at you. Don't discount the assistance that putting your back pack under your backside or between your ankles and the earth can have, when shooting from the kneeling positions. You can also place your pack or some similar object between your lap and your chest when shooting from the seated position. A partner can help, too. He can lie down and you can use his body as a front rest (with his permission of course) from the prone position.

THE SHOOTING BENCH

Simply put, you do not need one. Stay away from them. They will become a crutch that will promote bad habits and give you a false impression of your shooting abilities. Unless you are physically unable to shoot from the prone position, you'll never need a shooting bench.

Shooting around barricades is common in tactical situations, competition, and even when hunting. You'll need to lean out to the left or right to do this without exposing too much of yourself for the bad guy or the animal. You should practice shooting around barricades from all positions.

It is critical that you learn to use all the basic shooting positions, because it is likely you will have to use an unconventional position at some time. Knowing how to use the basic positions correctly will help you adapt to the strange positions (above and below) from which you might have to shoot.

Instead of the conventional support handhold (left), some shooters like to use the magazine well of the AR as a vertical forward grip for the support hand (right).

CHAPTER 14

TRAINING AND PRACTICE DRILLS

The following drills are just a few you can use to develop your shooting skills with an AR. These are drills I have used to improve my own shooting, and I've also used when instructing others. A benefit of these drills is that they offer a scoring mechanism, so you can keep track of your progress and evaluate your abilities. If you can meet the standards for a particular drill, you can consider your performance better than average, if not reasonably good.

BASIC PRONE

This is a basic sight alignment and trigger control drill, one designed to reinforce the basic principles of marksmanship. When you first conduct this drill, run it at 50 yards. When you can complete the drill miss free at that distance, increase the range to 100 yards. (If you are shooting an AR with open sights, work at 25 and 50 yards.) Concentrate on the basics of your position—breathing, sight alignment, and trigger control—and, at first, go at your own pace. There's no reason to try to complete this drill within the time limit if you cannot complete it while taking all the time you need.

Start in the prone position with the rifle loaded and the safety on. At the start signal,

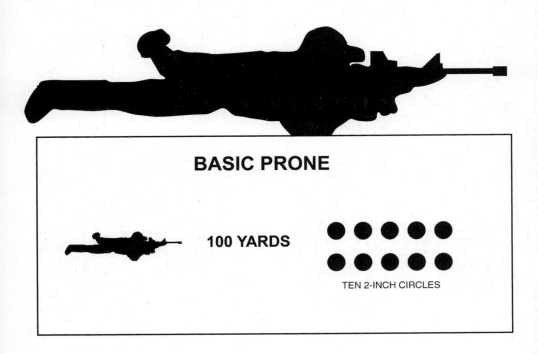

BASIC PRONE

100 YARDS

TEN 2-INCH CIRCLES

fire one shot each at 10 different two-inch Birchwood Casey Shoot-N-C circles placed at 50 yards. Each hit is worth 10 points and the goal is to get 10 hits—100 points—within 60 seconds. Subtract 10 points for every miss and one point for every second over 60 seconds. Once you successfully complete the drill without any misses at the 50-yard range, move the targets out to 100 yards.

PRACTICAL PRONE PRECISION DRILL

The purpose of this drill is to establish that you can make precision shots at various ranges; you'll have to compensate for bullet trajectory. This can be done by holding high or low, depending on how your rifle is sighted in. You can also click-in the trajectory compensation with the target turrets on your rifle scope or you might employ a ballistic reticle with additional aiming points for each distance.

You'll need three Birchwood Casey 5½-inch Shoot-N-C circle targets, one each placed at 100, 200, and 300 yards. (If you are shooting an AR with open sights, adjust the distance to the targets to 50, 100, and 150 yards.) Start in the prone position with the rifle loaded and the safety on. You can use a bipod or sandbags as a front rest, but nothing but body parts as a rear rest.

At the start signal, fire one shot at the 100-yard target, two shots at the 200-yard target, three shots at the 300-yard target, and then four more shots at the 100-yard target. The goal is to obtain all 10 hits within 30 seconds for a total score of 100 points. Subtract 10 points for every miss and one point for every second over 60 seconds.

Regardless how your AR is sighted in, the bullet's point of impact (POI) will be different than your point of aim (POA) at each range. The key to completing this drill within the time limit and obtaining hits at each range is to use the correct point of aim at each distance.

BASIC SITTING

Start in the seated position with the rifle loaded and the safety on. At the start signal,

PRACTICAL PRONE PRECISION

100 YARDS

200 YARDS

300 YARDS

THREE 5.5-INCH CIRCLES

fire one shot each at 10 different Birchwood Casey 5½-inch Snoot-N-C circle targets placed at 100 yards. (If you are shooting an AR with open sights, restrict the maximum range to 50 yards.) Each hit is worth 10 points and the goal is to get 10 hits within 60 seconds. Subtract 10 points for every miss and one point for every second over 60 seconds.

PRACTICAL SITTING DRILL

You'll need 5½-inch Birchwood Casey Shoot-N-C circle targets placed at 50, 75, and 100 yards. Start in the seated position with the rifle loaded and the safety on. At the start signal, fire one shot at the 50-yard target, two shots at the 75-yard target, three shots at the 100-yard target, and then four more shots at the 50-yard target. (If you are using an AR with iron sights, adjust the distance to the targets to 25, 50, and 75 yards.) The goal is to obtain all 10 hits (each hit is worth 10 points) within 30 seconds for a total score of 100 points. Subtract one point for every miss and one point for every second over 30 seconds.

BASIC SITTING

100 YARDS

TEN 5.5-INCH CIRCLES

PRACTICAL SITTING

50 YARDS ●

75 YARDS ●

100 YARDS ●

THREE 5.5-INCH CIRCLES

BASIC KNEELING

Start in the kneeling position with the rifle loaded and the safety on. At the start signal, fire one shot each at 10 different 5½-inch Birchwood Casey Snoot-N-C circle targets placed at 75 yards. Each hit is worth 10 points and the goal is to get 10 hits within 60 seconds. Subtract 10 points for every miss and one point for every second over 60 seconds.

PRACTICAL KNEELING DRILL

You'll need 5½-inch Birchwood Casey Shoot-N-C circle targets placed at 25, 50, and 75 yards. Start in the seated position with the rifle loaded and the safety on. At the start signal, fire one shot at the 25-yard target, two shots at the 50-yard target, three shots at the 75-yard target, and then four more shots at the 25-yard target. The goal is to obtain all 10 hits within 30 seconds for a total score of 100 points. Subtract 10 points for every miss and one point for every second over 30 seconds.

BASIC KNEELING

75 YARDS

TEN 5.5-INCH CIRCLES

PRACTICAL KNEELING

25 YARDS

50 YARDS

75 YARDS

THREE 5.5-INCH CIRCLES

BASIC STANDING

From the standing position, fire one shot each at 10 different 5½-inch Birchwood Casey Shoot-N-C circle targets placed at 50 yards. Each hit is worth 10 points and the goal is to get 10 hits within 60 seconds. Subtract 10 points for every miss and one point for every second over 60 seconds.

PRACTICAL STANDING DRILL

You'll need 5½-inch Birchwood Casey Shoot-N-C circle targets placed at 25, 50, and 75 yards. Start in the standing position, either in the indoor or outdoor ready position, with the rifle loaded and the safety on. At the start signal, fire two shots at the 25-yard target, two shots at the 50-yard target, two-shots at the 25-yard target, two shots at the 75-yard target, and two more shots at the 25-yard target. The goal is to obtain all 10 hits within 30 seconds for a total score of 100 points. Subtract 10 points for every miss and one point for every second over 30 seconds.

BASIC STANDING

50 YARDS

TEN 5.5-INCH CIRCLES

PRACTICAL STANDING

25 YARDS ●

50 YARDS ●

75 YARDS ●

THREE 5.5-INCH CIRCLES

"V" DRILL

You will need five Birchwood Casey Eze-Scorer TQ-19 (#37001) silhouette targets. Place one target at five yards, two at six yards, and two at seven yards. The target array should form a "V," with the five-yard target in the center flanked on each side by the six and seven yards targets, about a foot separating the targets laterally.

Start with the rifle in the outdoor ready position with the safety on. At the start signal, engage the targets as follows:

1. Center target: two shots
2. Left six-yard target: two shots.
3. Center target: two shots
4. Right six-yard target: two shots
5. Center target: two shots
6. Left seven-yard target: two shots.
7. Center target: two shots
8. Right seven-yard target: two shots.
9. Center target: two shots

You will fire 18 shots total and the goal is to obtain a hit in the light-grey zone of each silhouette target with each shot. Take your total time and add five seconds for every miss and one second for every hit in the dark-grey zone. If you get 17 light-grey zone hits in 6.28 seconds, your score would be 11.28 seconds. A great score is 5.00 or less, a good score is 10.00 or less and average is about 15.00.

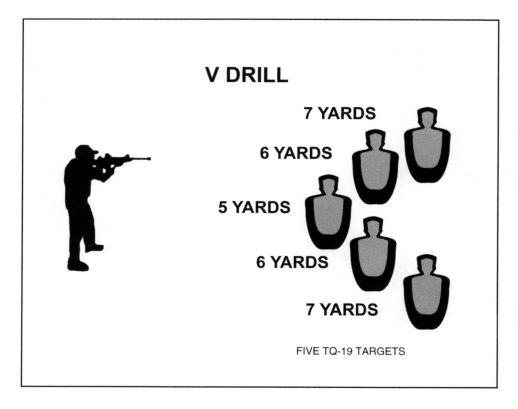

V DRILL

7 YARDS

6 YARDS

5 YARDS

6 YARDS

7 YARDS

FIVE TQ-19 TARGETS

MULTI-POSITION/QUALIFICATION-STYLE DRILLS

The following drills will test your ability to move between positions and to work from various ranges. From a training progression standpoint, it would be wise to master the preceding drills before attempting these.

SCOUT RIFLE WORKOUT

This drill is specifically designed for ARs or magazine-fed, scout-style, bolt-action rifles. Start standing with the rifle in the outdoor ready position. Place one 5½-inch Birchwood Casey Shoot-N-C circle target at 50 yards. At the signal, fire one shot from the standing position, one shot from kneeling, one shot from sitting, and one shot from prone. The goal is to keep all four shots inside the circle in less than 30 seconds. If you want to incorporate a reload

and additional shots, reload after the fourth shot (the shot from the prone position), and reverse the drill, firing four more shots with the last shot being from the standing position. The goal, then, is to keep all eight shots inside the five-inch circle in less than 60 seconds. Your score is your total time with 10 points added for every miss.

MODIFIED NAVY QUALIFICATION (MNQ) DRILL

Place a target with an eight-inch center zone, at 50 yards. (For more realism, place the eight-inch circle target on a Birchwood Casey Eze-Scorer B27 target or the Sharpshooter Corrugated Silhouette Die-Cut Kit target.) Load three magazines with five rounds each. At the firing line, assume the outdoor ready position with the rifle loaded and the safety on. When the buzzer sounds, fire five rounds from the standing position, reload, and fire five rounds from the kneel-

SCOUT RIFLE WORKOUT

50 YARDS

ONE 5.5 INCH TARGET

ing position. Reload again and fire your last five rounds from the prone position.

Your goal is to perform the drill with no misses in less than 25 seconds. Only hits in the eight-inch target zone count. You start with a score of zero and are penalized for misses and time over the par of 25 seconds. Add five points for every miss and two points for every second over 25 seconds. Subtract one point for every second under 25 seconds. For example, if you shoot the drill in 35 seconds with two misses, your score would be 30: 20 points for the 10 seconds over par and 10 points for the pair of misses. If you shoot the drill clean in 22 seconds, your score would be -3. Zero or less is a good score.

SAMPLE LAW ENFORCEMENT QUALIFICATION DRILL

For this drill, you will need one Birchwood Casey TQ-19 target and a 100-yard range. The course of fire requires 60 shots, and a passing score would be 80 percent or better. This means you must hit the silhouette target, within the light grey scoring area, no less than 48 times. Subtract two points for any shot that misses the complete silhouette.

DISTANCE: 100 YARDS/TOTAL SHOTS: 10
- Five shots from the prone position in 60 seconds.
- Five shots from the sitting position in 60 seconds.

DISTANCE: 75 YARDS/TOTAL SHOTS: 10
- Two shots from the standing position in five seconds.
- Two shots from the standing position in five seconds.
- Two shots from the kneeling position in five seconds.
- Two shots from the kneeling position in five seconds.
- Two shots from the kneeling position in five seconds.

DISTANCE: 50 YARDS/TOTAL SHOTS: 10
- Two shots from the standing position in five seconds.

MODIFIED NAVY QUALIFICATION (MNQ)

50 YARDS

ONE 8-INCH TARGET 16

- Two shots from the standing position in five seconds.
- One shot from the kneeling position in five seconds.
- One shot from the kneeling position in five seconds.
- One shot from the kneeling position in five seconds.
- One shot from the kneeling position in five seconds.
- One shot from the kneeling position in five seconds.
- One shot from the kneeling position in five seconds.

DISTANCE: 25 YARDS/TOTAL SHOTS: 6
- From behind cover, fire two shots over cover, two shots from the left side of cover, and two shots from the right side of cover within 30 seconds.

DISTANCE: 15 YARDS/TOTAL SHOTS: 4
- From the standing position, fire two shots, drop to kneeling, and fire two more shots within eight seconds.

DISTANCE: 7 YARDS/TOTAL SHOTS: 5
- From the standing position, fire two shots within three seconds.
- From the standing position, fire two shots to the body and one to the head within four seconds.

DISTANCE: 5 YARDS/TOTAL SHOTS: 5
- From the standing position, fire two shots within three seconds.
- From the standing position, fire two shots to the body and one to the head within four seconds.

CHAPTER 15

ARs AND NEW SHOOTERS

Somewhere along the line, someone who thought they knew a thing or two about teaching folks to shoot came up with the idea that it wasn't a good idea to let a new shooter start learning to shoot with a semi-automatic rifle. I guess there are a couple reasons for this assumption. Maybe they felt the new shooter would just go stupid and start pulling the trigger indiscriminately, shooting everything in sight. Or, maybe, they thought it would be hard for them to learn to shoot, because they could just shoot again quickly if they missed.

Some "rules," like don't start a new shooter out with a semi-automatic rifle, may sound like they make sense, but, when put to some scrutiny, actually make no sense at all. When teaching somebody, if the notion of having too much ammo at the student's disposal bothers you, then simply load only as many rounds in the magazine as you like. If you believe that having the ability to just keep pulling the trigger is a bad idea, look at it this way: with a semi-automatic, the new shooter can focus on shooting and not on working the action between shots.

Admittedly, I used to be of the no-semi-auto-for-beginners mindset, but, after some serious thought and experimentation, I believe that a semi-automatic might really be the *best* gun for a new shooter to learn with; with kids today, I'm almost sure of it. You see, back 50 years ago, the guns kids wanted to shoot were those that were popular, guns like lever-, bolt-, and pump-

There is nothing wrong, and maybe everything right, with teaching a new shooter to use a semi-automatic rifle like an AR.

A kid can be as responsible with an AR as they can with any firearm. The key is instruction, training, and education.

action rifles. Heck, it wasn't all that long ago that single-shot rifles were popular. Today, things have changed. Kids see ARs everywhere, including on TV and in video games—and, if *you* own an AR, they see *you* shoot it. The popularity of the AR makes it a rifle youngsters want to shoot, and the best way to learn to shoot is to shoot what you want to shoot.

I'm sure there are plenty of anti-gun people who would read that statement and become consumed with hate and rage and then declare me irresponsible. Those same anti-gun people have most likely never met someone like my son, who started shooting when he was four, killed a deer with an AR when he was seven, and continues to shoot

and hunt at every opportunity unless there's a basketball handy. He also plays those evil video games and is a well-mannered and good-hearted person.

Here's the thing, though, as a gun owner, you probably already know this. It's not about the type of gun, but, rather, the character of the person. The point of all this meandering is that starting a new shooter with an AR will not make them a evil person, nor will it produce an inherent desire to go out an gun down school children, theatergoers, or anyone else. Raise your kids right and it will all be okay.

Here's a perfect example. A good friend of mine called me a year ago and asked what rifle he should let his 10-year-old son learn to

ARs are very adaptable to the size of the shooter. This makes them a great first rifle.

shoot with, so that he could go deer hunting. The problem was that his 10-year-old son was small for his age. For someone to be able to shoot a rifle properly, the rifle needs to fit them, and all the so-called "youth rifles" on the market were still just too big for the friend's son.

For me, the answer to my friend's issue was an easy one. When my son was seven years old, we'd had the same problem. Now, the year before, when he had been six, a custom rifle builder had put together a very compact bolt-action rifle for him to try. It worked great, but I had to return that rifle,

so my son and I were left with a dilemma. Then, while sitting at my desk one day, daydreaming about this and that instead of writing, I looked over in the corner and noticed my AR leaning against the wall. The six-position adjustable stock was in its first setting, and I immediately realized that gun would be the perfect fit for him. A little practice, and with one shot he had his second deer.

I suggested my friend try his son out on an AR with a collapsible stock and, when he did, it worked out just as well as it had for my boy. In fact, his son used that rifle to

These ladies just graduated from a class at Gunsite, where they learned to operate and shoot an AR, some for the very first time.

take two deer that hunting season and then two more the next.

You see, an AR with a collapsible stock has a length of pull (LOP)—the distance from the trigger to the end of the stock—a full two inches shorter than most dedicated youth-sized centerfire rifles. This same logic regarding fit also applies to many women, who are often a bit shorter than the average guy most rifles are designed to fit. As another example, when my wife went to Gunsite with a group of ladies to learn how to shoot a rifle, she used an AR. She's only about five feet tall, and the AR with its collapsible stock fit her perfectly. And, as surprising as it may seem to some, she learned to shoot it very well, even though it was a semi-automatic.

Two final thoughts about the suitability of an AR to a new shooter deal with the gun's weight. A carbine-length AR can be

had that will weigh about six pounds. One issue new and especially young shooters have when first learning to shoot is their rifle's weight. When it comes to a centerfire rifle, six pounds is about as light as they get, unless you want to pay through the nose for a custom job. Also, most ARs are chambered for the .223 Remington cartridge, which delivers negligible recoil. Too much recoil is also a bad thing for a new shooter.

This is all good news, especially if you already own an AR. If yours does not have an adjustable buttstock or it's a bit heavy, the modularity of the platform will allow you to manipulate the AR so that it is indeed just right for a new shooter.

One thing I will agree with, when it comes to new shooters, is that, in every case, the .22 LR rifle cartridge is where you should start. Again, with the AR, this is not a problem. You have two solid options.

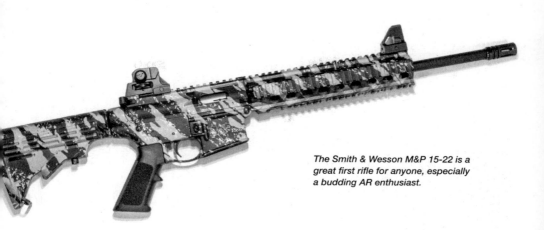

The Smith & Wesson M&P 15-22 is a great first rifle for anyone, especially a budding AR enthusiast.

First, you can purchase a dedicated .22 LR upper for your AR. This is a complete upper assembly that replaces the centerfire upper assembly on your gun. This allows the new shooter to learn and practice with a rifle identical in feel and function to the centerfire rifle to which they will eventually graduate. In addition to the learning part, over the long haul, this dedicated .22 LR upper will get a lot of use for skill sustainment and, likely, recreational shooting. If you or your new shooter are or plan to be a hunter, such a configuration will also give you a great small-game rifle.

I'm sure you've heard the saying, "Beware the man with one gun." I'm not sure many of us want to have only one gun, but this cliché came about for a reason. The man who has only one gun should know how to shoot that gun really well, because it is the only gun he ever shoots. Think about it this way: If you borrow a friend's car, you can still drive it, but likely not as comfortably or with the precision with which you drive your own.

If you install a dedicated .22 LR upper on your AR, the lower receiver stays the same, including the magazine release, safety selector switch, and the bolt lock/release. More importantly, the trigger stays the same, and knowing the feel and function of your trigger is a critical part of shooting with precision. Essentially, when your kids, your wife, or you shoot an AR with a dedicated .22 LR upper, you're all doing exactly the same things you will be doing when you all shoot the AR with a centerfire upper receiver installed—but it'll cost a lot less and make a lot less noise.

The second option, when bringing a new shooter on board with an AR, is to purchase a complete AR *dedicated* to the .22 LR. Several manufacturers offer these rifles. Some companies, like Mossberg and Ruger, offer their standard .22 LR semi-automatic rifle in AR dress. These dressed-up rifles may not operate or look exactly like an AR, but they are close and, so, can be used to teach the proper manual of arms with the AR.

I've experimented with most of these dedicated .22 LR ARs and, for the most part, they all work. However, hands down, I feel the S&W M&P 15-22 is the clear winner. Not only does it look and feel exactly like an AR-15, all the controls are in the exact same place and they all work exactly the same as they would on the centerfire variation. The downside, of course, is that, when you practice with this rifle in its dedicated

It's important that a new shooter be able to operate and physically support the rifle they're shooting. It's just as important that they are able to load the magazines.

.22 LR form, you're pulling a trigger that is different than the trigger on a centerfire AR. If you have both rifles, you can fix this inconsistency by installing identical after-market triggers, like those from Timney, in both rifles. Smith & Wesson makes the M&P 15-22 in a wide range of configurations and, while they are not as adaptable to accessories and add-ons as their centerfire counterparts, they are accurate and very dependable.

The other big advantage the S&W M&P 15-22 offers is that it's made of polymer, which means that, at roughly four pounds total, it's a full two pounds lighter than even the lightest centerfire AR you can find. For new shooters, young or old, this is a great thing. They will not experience arm strain while shooting and, if they are really young, the rifle is just that much easier for them to hold onto all the way around, and that means an added measure of safety.

The procedure for teaching a new shooter to shoot AR is really no different than it would be for them to learn to shoot any other rifle. The ultimate goal should be for them to be able to complete the drills listed in Chapter 14. Still, if the new shooter is young or has never shot at all before, here are some training suggestions you might want to consider:

- Start off new shooters at a shooting bench or, if they are comfortable with

As a new shooter becomes more proficient with the AR, they can begin to shoot in body positions that are further away from the ground. Remember, the closer you are to the ground, the easier it is to get hits, so prone is an ideal position from which to begin the new shooter.

it, from the prone position. In either case, use sandbags to stabilize the front and rear of the AR.

- Let the student shoot enough to learn the basics of proper sight alignment, trigger control, and follow-through.
- Once they have shown a mastery of those basic skills at close range, say, 15 yards, increase the distance to 30 and, ultimately, 50 yards.
- With a shooter consistently getting good hits at 50 yards (putting all their shots in a five-inch circle from the bench or the prone position over the sandbags), move them to the prone un-supported position and pull the target

back to 15 yards or so. Let the shooter work there way out to 50 yards again, with the goal of keeping all shots inside a five-inch target.

- Pull the target back to 15 yards again, move the shooter to the seated position and follow the same process. Continue this regimen for the kneeling and standing positions.
- Once a shooter can demonstrate proficiency with the .22 LR AR, and if their arm strength will allow, graduate them up to the centerfire and start all over. If they start flinching or having issues, go back to the .22 LR AR until the problem is corrected.

Kids can learn to shoot an AR at a very young age and well enough to hunt with one ethically and responsibly.

One thing I would strongly suggest with a new shooter, young or old, is to frequently include reactive targets like steel, balloons, crackers, or even rotten fruit. Shooting paper is boring for adults and even more so for kids. When you're learning something new, it's great to get some immediate gratification that you are, in fact, doing it right. My son is now 13 and he still talks about the lollipop he busted when he was six.

Remember to take the opportunity during each training session to instill the importance of a proper manual of arms. Set up stoppages with empty cases and let the new shooter clear them. Teach them the proper methods of indoor and outdoor carry. Show them how to load, unload, and field strip the AR, and show them how to perform a function check. The ability to understand these things and to perform them takes some of the mystique of the firearm out of the equation and, with that gone, the new shooter can focus on learning to shoot. Sure, you can learn to shoot with a variety of different firearms, but I have two little girls and a Smith & Wesson M&P 15-22. That's what they will learn on, and I bet that, just like their mommy, when they're old enough to graduate to a centerfire rifle, it will be an AR, too.

An AR is one of the few centerfire or rimfire rifles that can grow with a kid. It's just one more reason it is the most versatile and adaptable firearms system of all time.

CHAPTER 16

BUILD YOUR OWN AR

For most who enjoy firearms, there's a common progression of interest and the activities in which they participate. The act of shooting, generally considered the most fun thing to do with a gun, comes first, and then, as the interest in shooting expands, so does the interest in learning more about firearms. This often leads to research about and the purchase of accessories. It's not uncommon for shooters to soon become involved in formal competition, so they can test their skills against that of their friends and others who are considered to be top shots. Of course, there is hunting.

Most anyone who can operate a toaster or a DVD player can build their own AR, and such a build can be expected to shoot very well.

For a lot of gun owners, it stops there. For others, the desire to become more at one with their gun continues, and they begin to craft their own ammunition. Home gunsmithing is also popular, not only because it allows shooters to tweak their firearms, but because it helps them better understand their guns and gives them a way to enjoy firearms at home in the evening or during other times when they cannot shoot.

Of course, there's also the customization aspect that goes along with learning to gunsmith. For the true firearms enthusiast, there's nothing that will rival a custom-built firearm. With most traditional rifles, a custom gun requires the talents of a good gunsmith who knows how to apply trade secrets to an action, barrel, stock, and trigger. These skills are not cheap

and, for many, a custom bolt-action rifle is beyond their maximum financial range. The modularity of the AR platform and the vast diversity of parts and accessories have changed all that. With just a modicum of mechanical ability, you can build your own AR piece by piece. It is a very rewarding endeavor and one that is also extremely educational.

I could wax on about how rewarding this process can be, but I believe a friend and his story about his son who wanted to hunt deer is a much better way to demonstrate how this process works and how it can be instrumental to the overall aspects of shooting and fun. Let us not forget that even though firearms can serve a multitude of very important tasks, for most shooters, they simply provide enjoyment and entertainment.

One advantage of building your own AR is that you can configure it exactly like you want it. It's also a way to save a little cash.

Jack Wanted to Hunt Deer *By Chris Ellis*

Jack wanted to hunt deer.

He wanted to be able to go to deer camp and shoot deer like the other, older members of his family. He had heard the stories told around the campfire, and he had listened to the other kids in his circle of friends talking about hunting. He, too, wanted to actively participate in the sport of deer hunting and feel the pride of filling the family's freezer full of fresh venison to share at the dinner table.

The only problems for Jack were his size and his anxiety over heavy recoiling rifles. Jack was small for his age, tipping the scale at 80 pounds with his backpack full of schoolbooks. Sure, we could have waited until he was a little bigger and more mature, but he seriously wanted to be part of the hunt and enjoy the gifts of nature's bounty.

Momentum and attitude were with us. I was determined not to curb Jack's drive or enthusiasm just because I couldn't find a deer rifle to suit his needs. But, after trying various rifles, including bolt-actions, lever guns, and even single-shots, we still couldn't find a rifle that fit him perfectly. The heavy ones didn't kick as much, but he couldn't hold them steady enough to hit where he aimed. The short-barreled rifles were easier to handle, but the muzzle blast, being so much closer to face, caused him to jerk the trigger in anticipation of the fireball at the end of the barrel.

With the help of a former police and military firearms instructor at the range, it was determined that my 11-year-old son should be leaning towards the AR platform for his first deer rifle, and for a few simple reasons. First and most importantly, the collapsible stock adjusted to fit him perfectly. The heavy barrel allowed him the benefit of keeping his sights on the target without much wobble, and the buffer spring reduced felt recoil down to something that was comfortable for him to shoot. Additionally, the AR, as seen through Jack's eyes, was really, really cool.

Once we determined his preference towards AR rifles, I heeded the advice of a friend to build a rifle, instead of purchasing one. In fact, this wise shooter told me that Jack should build his own AR. He said that not only would Jack learn about the rifle and its parts, he would have fun picking out the various components. In the end, he'd have a strong connection to his first deer rifle and pride in the fact that he'd built it.

The build was actually simple! We started with a stripped lower receiver, several bags of parts, a Timney trigger, and a few punches. We watched the Bushmaster Armorer's DVD and, with the help of an AR schematic, we learned—together—what each little spring, plunger, and part was called and how to install them. More importantly, we learned how to replace these if they broke. After the lower receiver was assembled, we opted to purchase a complete upper assembly with a target-grade barrel.

Jack killed two deer that fall with his rifle. He now carries a field kit full of extra parts in his hunting backpack and can field strip and clean his rifle like Forrest Gump. He's also been talking about becoming a gunsmith when he gets older. If you happen to drop by the house on a crisp fall evening, he will gladly show you his AR rifle and proudly tell you that he provided the table fare for the evening's meal with it. Jack built an AR and Jack got what he wanted: he is now a deer hunter.

Of course, not everyone wants to hunt deer. Some shooters just want an AR and would like to experience building it themselves. Regardless the reasons, it should be clear that doing it yourself could instill a distinct level of pride and accomplishment. It's no different than other projects you might tackle around the home, like changing the oil in your truck, building a deck, or cutting down a dead tree near the house. Do-it-yourself projects have always been popular, because folks like to say, "I did that myself."

The approach Chris took with his son, Jack, is the most common. Assembling the lower receiver for an AR isn't all that difficult and requires only a few special tools. The build can be accomplished in

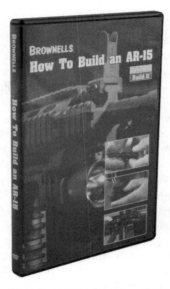

Instructional videos, like this one from Brownells, cover all the aspects of building your own AR.

Though there are some special tools needed for building an AR at home, they are not very expensive, and some companies like Brownells even offer them in a kit.

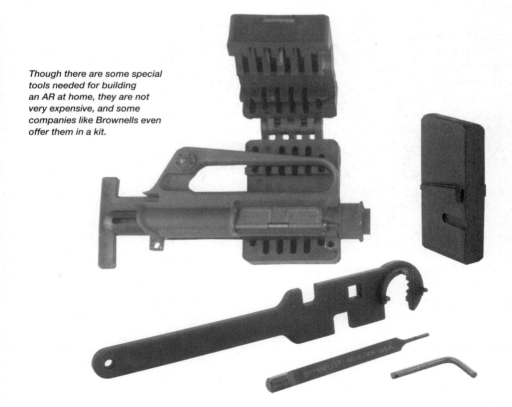

an evening, and you can do it right on the kitchen table. You'll learn a great deal during the process, because, as you put the parts together, you will develop a better understanding of how they work together.

Another approach is to also build the complete upper assembly. The upper assembly on an AR is really where all the diversity hinges, and here you will get to make any crucial decisions about how you want your AR to be configured. You'll have to choose the type of upper you want, the cartridge you want it to work with, the type and length of barrel, the gas system, and the handguards. The options will seem so endless you might think there is no way you can make up your mind. The trick is to be patient and take the time to consider the things you hope to do with your AR and then how to best set it up for that type of shooting.

The best way to tackle the actual assembly is to find a DVD or book that details the assembly procedure. Chris and Jack utilized the Bushmaster DVD. As for a book, I'd suggest Patrick Sweeney's *Gunsmithing the AR-15* (www.gundigeststore.com). Actually, it's not a bad idea to utilize both resources, but, as much as I like the DVD, the book provides more technical information and is a great, easy to turn to resource.

Humans like to make things. Man, woman, or child, creating stuff is human nature. Our ability to craft things is what sets us apart from all the other animals on this planet. Sure, some animals make nests or dens, but humans create all sorts of cool stuff. We take pride in our ability to create things as

A variety of books and DVDs on building ARs are available from various sources, including www.gundigeststore.com.

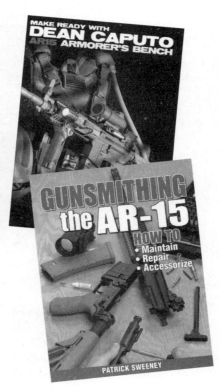

Brownells has an interactive website to help you configure a new AR at home.

simple as a Crayon-colored picture to things as complex as a skyscraper. Us older folks will remember our first set of Lincoln Logs, and what kid or adult hasn't spent half a day building something with Legos?

When I was in my teens, muzzleloading rifle kits were very popular. It was cool to build a gun and then shoot or even hunt with it. Those muzzleloading rifles and the kit guns that were once so popular, and while still sometimes available, have been replaced with by the AR. Assembling the AR's 100 parts might seem a daunting task, but, when you think about it, most model car or airplane kits have just as many parts. Of course, you can purchase many AR components pre-assembled. The only thing the novice AR builder will need before they begin are instructions. Unlike model airplane kits, AR parts or kits do not come with directions.

For more than 70 years, Brownells (www.brownells.com) has been the go-to place for firearms parts and gunsmithing tools. Brownells has developed a website called www.AR15builder.com. As a companion to this portal, where you can virtually assemble your AR-15 dream gun, Brownells put together a set of videos and instructions on how to do it.

As cool as these videos are, though, some folks like an instruction book when working on a project like this, so Brownells also offers several books, such as *The Complete AR-15 Assembly Guide* and *Build Your Own AR-15*. Both will walk you through the process step by step. Depending on the level of assembly you want to attempt, some special tools can be a big help, and Brownells has taken the complexity out of trying to decide which tools you need by putting together what it calls the "AR-15 Critical

An AR build project can be a fun endeavor for the family and is a great way for all to learn how the AR works.

Tool Kit," which contains the primary and essential tools you need to assemble an AR-15.

By using the Brownells www.AR15builder.com website, you can configure your build one part at a time. The application catalogs your parts, and you can order everything from a complete AR build assembly or merely the parts to convert or customize your current AR. You can even use the site as a drawing board to configure your AR, and then part it out from other manufacturers. A number of manufacturers offer upper and lower receivers, as well as just parts.

Larry Weeks, with Brownells, believes most people are customizing ARs these days, as opposed to building them from scratch. Some may have an AR they want to modernize or configure for a specific purpose, so they build up a new upper receiver or modify the lower. This is a good way to start, but very likely you'll have so much fun you'll end up starting a new project gun from scratch.

Assembling an AR is a fun project and can include about any family member above the age of six or so. Remember, building an AR isn't just about putting parts together. Half the fun is selecting the different parts, such as the grip, stock, and handguard you want. The AR is the only rifle you can custom build to suit your needs, right on your kitchen table, in one afternoon. If you're a hunter, you can then use that AR to put some savory food on that same table this fall, just like Chris and Jack did.

CHAPTER 17

HANDLOADING FOR THE AR

When handloading for an AR, there are some considerations you have to make that you might be able to overlook if you were loading for a bolt-action rifle. Let's take a look at what it takes to successfully load specifically for the AR. Too, let's assume you have a working knowledge of reloading practices; you know how to operate a press, either progressive or single-stage, and you under-

You can save money and even further increase the versatility of your AR by handloading.

stand the process and tools involved and the safety practices inherent with handling powders and primers.

In handloading for the AR, the first consideration is in sizing the case. Since semi-automatic firearms like the AR lack the capability of being operated with extreme force, cases need to be full-length resized. This ensures that the case will slip fully into the chamber with no more force than can be imparted on the case as provided by the recoil spring. If the ammunition in your AR is dirty or if it has only been neck sized, the buffer spring may not have the necessary force to push it completely into the chamber. Additionally, if you're going to load ammo for an AR, it's suggested that you use small base dies. A small base die imparts a bit more sizing into the operation than a standard die. Still, I have to tell you that I have loaded

If you're new to handloading, consider the RCBS instructional DVD or seek out the advice of an experienced handloader.

When handloading for any AR, it's always a good idea to use a small base sizing die.

for a lot of ARs with both small base and standard dies and have yet to see where the standard dies are an issue, though I've had acquaintances who have had problems. So, as a rule of thumb, it's not a bad idea to use a small base die, when loading for an AR.

There is another issue that can arise when loading for an AR, specifically if the cartridge is based on the .223 Remington/5.56 NATO case. You see, some .223 Remington and almost all 5.56 NATO cases have primers that have been crimped in place. It is impossible to re-prime these cases until that crimp has been removed. You can circumvent this problem by only using brass that has not had the primer

You need to start with clean brass. A case tumbler is a must-have tool.

The RCBS Primer Pocket Swager Tool will remove the crimp from large and small primer cups.

crimped in place, but this can limit your access to brass. Some shooters like to search the shooting range looking for brass for cartridges they load. Nothing wrong with that, but, if you want to use any and all brass you scrounge, you'll need to be prepared to remove the crimp from some of it.

This same issue, by the way, also applies to some 6.8 SPC, .300 Blackout and .308 brass. Some factory ammo for these cartridges will have crimped primers and some will not. It's something not all that easy to spot with an untrained eye; even with experience detecting crimped primers, you can miss a few. When you try to prime a case for which the previous primer was crimped in place, you will feel a lot of resistance, but still may manage to stick the primer partway in the case. This can lock up a progressive press, a single-stage press, and even a hand-priming tool.

Removing a crimp in a case isn't that difficult, but it can be time consuming, particularly if you're working with an unknown batch of brass, because you will need to check each primer pocket. RCBS makes a Primer Pocket Reamer tool that

You can use the RCBS Primer Swaging Tool to check to see if a primer pocket needs to be swaged.

If you run into a case with a crimped primer pocket while loading, it could lock up your press and even your hand priming tool. It is better to sort this out before the actual loading beings.

works with a single-stage press. It comes with the necessary accessories to remove the crimp for a small or large primer and does so with perfection. You can also use the tool to quickly check each primer pocket during the brass preparation phase.

BRASS PREPARATION

Brass preparation is always critical, when it comes to handloading. Your brass needs to be clean so that it chambers smoothly and, ideally, it should be of the uniform length or at least of a length under the allowable maximum. A case trimmer will allow you to trim each piece of brass to a minimum length.

Trimming cases can help with accuracy, but this facet of handloading in the AR can also be a safety issue. When you are handloading bullets of 100 grains or more,

they need a certain amount of neck tension to keep them seated. ARs slam cartridges out of the magazine and into the chamber. When the bullet impacts the feed ramp, it can be pushed back into the case. Also, when the bullet enters the chamber, if the force pushing it there is great enough, the bullet can eke forward slightly. Inconsistent bullet seating depth can be detrimental to accuracy, but, if a bullet eases out too close to the rifling or actually comes into contact with the rifling, pressures can rise drastically. The cure is crimping the bullet into the case. In most instances, this isn't an issue with the .223 Remington/5.56 NATO cartridge, due to the less than 100-grain weight of the bullets those cartridges use, but, if there isn't sufficient neck tension on the bullets you do choose to use, it can still occur. Ideally, and as a general rule, you

Trimming brass is time consuming, but brass uniformity is critical, when it comes to accuracy and crimping bullets.

should crimp all bullets in place when loading for an AR.

There are two types of crimps, the roll crimp and the taper crimp. A roll crimp generally requires a special roll-crimping die and is performed in an operation separate from seating the bullet. Taper crimping can be done with the same die used to seat the bullet, either when the bullet is seated or in a separate step. RCBS seating dies that are capable of taper crimping are marked "TC."

Crimping the bullet in place carries with it a small complication. In order to crimp the bullet in place at the same time you're seating the bullet, or to do so in a separate step with any speed and consistency, all your cases need to be the same length. This means that to load the safest and most accurate ammo you can, you will need to check case length and trim accordingly during the brass prep phase. There is another option, and it's one I have used this with good success on bullets weighing less than 150 grains. When you size your cases, remove the expander ball from the die. The expander ball expands the case mouth back to the proper size after the sizing die has sized it. The amount of expansion is small, but it is enough to cause a reduction in neck tension, depending on how thick the brass is in the neck of the cartridge. However, this expansion by the expander ball isn't *necessary*. You can still seat a bullet with ease. That being said, if you're loading flat-based bullets, you will need to give each case a decent chamfer on the inside of the case mouth, in order to get the bullet started. If you have trimmed your brass, this is something you will have had to do anyway.

Regardless the AR you are loading for, the overall cartridge length must not be too long to work in the magazine.

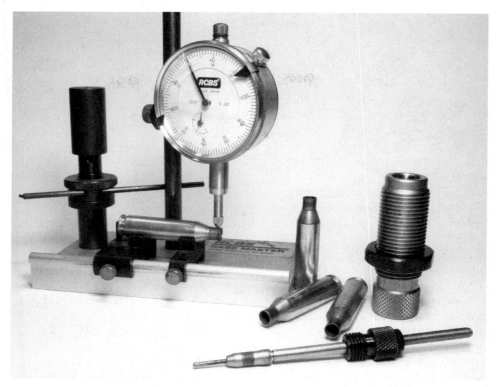

Removing the expander ball from your sizing die will allow your cases to have more neck tension. It also helps to keep necks straighter, which is something you can check with the RCBS Casemaster.

Beyond these case prep issues, hand-loading for an AR is really no different than loading for any other cartridge. By performing the case-prep steps as I've just discussed them, you are, essentially, making ammo the same way that factories make ammo. The only other aspect of loading for an AR that is a bit different is timing.

As you know by now, the AR relies on gas generated by the burning powder to drive the operating system, whether it's a piston or gas impingement system. The pressure of this gas needs to fall within a certain window, in order for the AR to run smoothly. Too much or not enough gas creates timing issues that can lead to failures to fully cycle, as well as another phenomena called "case head swipe."

Case head swipe (CHS) with AR rifles is similar to, but not the same as, ejector marks seen on cartridge case heads fired in bolt rifles. When a high- or overpressure load is fired in a bolt-action rifle, the brass of the cartridge case flows into the recess of the ejector. The result is a bright mark on the head of the cartridge case. With CHS, the marks come from the ejector and extractor cutouts in the bolt face. It can be an indication of high pressure, that your rifle is not timed for the load you're shooting, or both.

When a cartridge is fired in an AR, the case expands and fuses itself to the chamber until the pressure drops. When that happens, the brass springs back nearly to unfired size. As the bullet passes down the barrel, it is

Here you can see varying degrees of CHS on these .30 Remington AR cases. The case on the left is normal, the next case has minimal CHS, and the third from the left has moderate CHS. The far right case has excessive CHS and a popped primer.

followed by gas—pressure. When the bullet passes the gas port, gas leaks into the port and is diverted to the gas key on the bolt carrier. But some pressure still remains until the bullet exits the barrel. The time it takes the bullet to travel from gas port to muzzle exit is called "dwell time."

Carbine- and rifle-length barrels have different gas tub lengths to optimize dwell time. If too much pressure passes through the gas tube, or if the dwell time is too long, the bolt carrier starts reward travel *before* the case lets go of the chamber. As gas forces the bolt carrier back, the bolt begins to rotate and move forward in the bolt carrier while the cartridge case is still under pressure and being pushed back against the bolt face; in a perfect world, the bolt lugs do not start to unlock— rotate—until the bullet has left the muzzle and the case has released its hold inside the chamber. That premature rotation is what causes CHS. In essence, the edges of the ejector and extractor cutouts in the bolt face scrape the hot and malleable case head and create bright marks, even burrs.

What causes excessive dwell time? Often it's when pressures remain similar,

but bullet weight is increased. I was testing a DPMS AR-10 in .308 Winchester and, when I switched from 150-grain to 180-grain factory loads, minimal CHS appeared. The slower velocity of the heavier bullet increased the dwell time, causing the bolt carrier to move too soon. Yes, minimal CHS can be a sign of high pressure, but more than likely it indicates a timing issue; certain loads simply cause the action to begin working too soon.

Because of their different pressure curves, different powders can also cause CHS. I was loading the .30 Remington AR with Ramshot Xterminator powder and 110-grain bullets. When I reached a muzzle velocity of 2,860 fps, CHS appeared. I switched to Alliant Reloader 10X and achieved the same velocity without CHS. I then tried Hodgdon's H322 and pushed the 110-grain bullet to just over 3,000 fps, again without CHS. Yet all these powders have similar burn rates.

If you're seeing moderate to excessive CHS, there's a problem. It could be an ammo problem, a gun problem, or both. Is it a serious problem? Barring another sign of high pressure, such as excessive veloci-

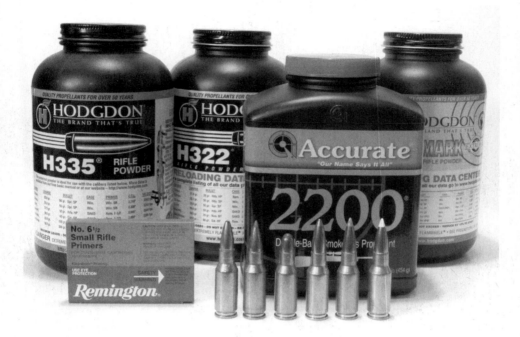

Some AR cartridges only work well with a few powders, while others like the .223 Remington will work with a much wider selection.

ties for your barrel length and failures to feed where the bolt carrier cycles too fast for the magazine to feed up the next cartridge, minimal CHS is *probably* not dangerous. Keep in mind that brass from some manufacturers may be softer than others, and this can exaggerate CHS. It's fairly common for many AR-15s and AR-10s to show minimal CHS with some factory (read, pressure-safe) loads.

The ominous blown primer is generally considered a true sign of high pressure, but, according to Nosler, this is not always the case with an AR. In severe cases of improperly timed weapons, the same circumstances that can cause CHS allow the primer cup to move rearward in the primer pocket and the seal can be compromised. The primer doesn't actually fall out until the case is ejected and, when that happens, the primer usually ends up lying in the trigger housing.

Again, the popped primer may not be a true indication of high pressure, but it is a definite sign of a problem that needs to be addressed through ammunition selection and/or by altering the timing of the gun.

For what it's worth, I treat a popped primer as a sign of high pressure and, for safety's sake, suggest you do the same. You can tell the difference in a blown and a popped primer. A blown primer will fit back into the primer pocket of the case it came out of, because the primer pocket has expanded due to high pressure. A popped primer will not fit back into the primer pocket, because the pocket didn't expand, it just lost its grip on the primer when the bolt face moved to the rear too soon.

Case head swipe can appear on just some of the ejected cases out of the same lot of factory or handloaded ammunition, because peak pressure and velocity can

You can create a wide assortment of loads for AR cartridges. In the case of the .300 AAC Blackout, bullets can vary in weight from 110 to 220 grains. These loads will all generate different pressures and dwell times.

vary a great deal between rounds out of the same lot—as much as 4,000 psi and over 100 fps. One thing I like about the .30 Remington AR is that, generally, standard velocity deviations are in the single digits, so, if case head swipe appears on one case, it will likely appear on all cases from the same lot. This is a good reason to select loads that produce very consistent velocities, regardless the cartridge or rifle they are fired in.

Excessive CHS can mar case heads so badly they'll not fit into the shellholder when handloading. You can easily fix this with a flat file, but the real solution is to cure the problem. Back the powder charge down or switch powders and maybe even primers. I would like to tell you that either a slower *or* faster burning powder will cure this, but I've seen it eliminated with both.

Another way to correct for case head swipe is to alter the timing of the AR. You can do this by switching to a heavier recoil spring, weighting the buffer, installing an adjustable gas block, or any combination of these. However, don't assume that because certain loads show no case head swipe in one AR that they'll perform the same in

another. The length and size of the gas tubes and the size of the gas ports can be different gun to gun, and the buffer spring's strengths and buffer's weights can vary, too.

When I see anything beyond minimal CHS on any of my AR handloads, I fix the problem by fixing the load. With a factory stock rifle frequently showing *moderate to excessive* case head swipe with factory ammo that's using common, mid-range bullet weights, I would send it to the manufacturer and let them correct the issue. (Remember, factory ammo is loaded to work in any firearm, so commercial ammunition makers apply that consideration because they don't have any idea what type of firearm a consumer will be putting their ammo into.) For guns you've built in your garage, you'll have to sort out the timing or the proper ammo on your own.

For what it's worth, I talked with a lot of smart folks from bullet, ammunition, and firearm manufacturers while researching the CHS phenomena. I got a lot of different and sometimes conflicting answers and several, "That's weird" comments. The information here represents the general consensus. *If*

Case prep can be time consuming. That's why electronic tools are a good idea, especially if you are going to load a lot of ammo.

Due to the wide assortment of small and light .30-caliber bullets, you can create .300 AAC Blackout loads that are versatile and useful, but that will also chamber in a .223 Remington. That's a significant safety issue, one you should be distinctly aware of if you're shooting either or both rounds. Sort your brass carefully and proceed with caution.

you're seeing moderate to excessive case head swipe fix the problem. Get the timing right by altering the gun or the ammo. Just like a 65 Corvette, an AR needs to be timed right to run right.

Another warning that needs mentioning relates to the .300 AAC Blackout cartridge. This cartridge uses the same base case as the .223 Remington, but the round is much shorter. An empty .300 AAC Blackout case will easily chamber in a .223 Remington AR. Most .300 AAC Blackout factory ammunition is loaded with really long bullets or bullets seated out far enough to prevent the cartridge from being chambered in a .223 Remington. In these cases, the bullet hits the point in the .223 Remington chamber where it shrinks for the shoulder. If the bolt goes forward with enough force and if there isn't sufficient neck tension, the bullet in the .300 AAC Blackout case can be driven back into the case far enough that the cartridge *will*

Tip: ARs are, for the most part, volume-fire weapons. No one wants to go to the range and shoot only one box of 20 rounds. To take advantage of the savings you can appreciate through handloading, you'll also want to save time, and the best way to do that is with a progressive press. Unless you're just loading a few rounds to hunt with or like to experiment with different loads in your AR, consider learning to use a progressive press. With a little practice, you'll be able to punch out 1,000 rounds in one evening.

chamber in a .223 Remington AR. You can also force a .300 AAC Blackout cartridge to chamber in a .223 Remington by beating hard on the forward assist. If this happens and you pull the trigger, do not expect your AR to survive the resulting loud bang—and

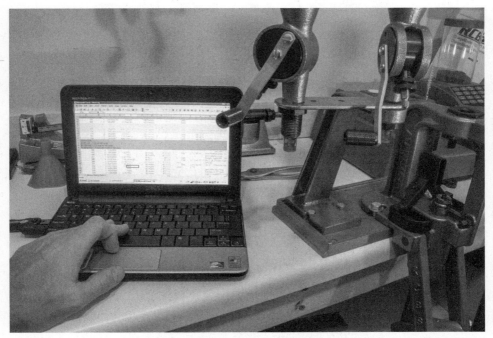

Keep accurate and detailed handloading records. Do not discount the use of a computer for storing your data.

you will be lottery ticket lucky if you survive the incident without a serious injury.

This information is important because many who own an AR in .300 AAC Blackout also own another upper or another AR in .223 Remington/5.56 NATO. Ammo can get mixed up and a problem can occur. You could also create a handload with a very short bullet for the .300 AAC Blackout that would easily chamber in the .223 Remington. One of my favorite .300 AAC Blackout loads utilizes the short 110-grain round-nose Speer Deep Curl bullet—and that load will slip right into a .223 Remington AR's chamber.

As with all things firearms and handloading, be careful! This means keeping track of your ammo. Don't mix it up. Keep ammo separated, when shooting multiple calibers during the same session. Follow the load data provided by the bullet and powder manufacturers and have at least a basic understanding of how individual powders and primers work. For instance, the very small cases used by some AR-15 cartridges work best when filled with fast-burning powders. At the same time, that's a combination that

reacts very quickly to small changes in powder charge; in some cases, just a few tenths of a grain of powder will punch your load over the maximum allowable average pressure. Your AR may fire one, ten, or a hundred of these loads just fine, but stress on a firearm is cumulative and, eventually, you're going to see a problem with excessive wear, or even a catastrophic failure.

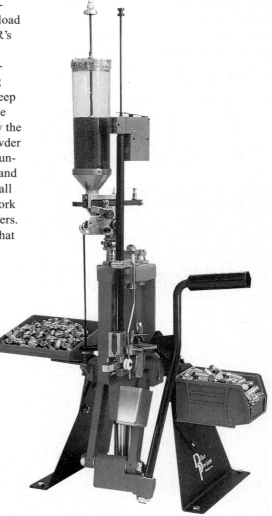

If you are going to shoot your AR a lot, consider a progressive press that will allow you to load a lot of ammo in a hurry.

CHAPTER 18

LEGALITY

There is a great deal of confusion nationwide, regarding the legality of the AR. Some shooters believe they are illegal to own, while others believe there are certain jurisdictions where you cannot own an AR. Admittedly, this is somewhat understandable. The AR receives an immense amount of news coverage, most of which seems to support the anti-gun agenda.

The fact that laws in a variety of states constantly change and that sometimes a proposed law is mistaken as actual law further complicates the issue. You would think that, as popular as the AR-style platform is, there would be an easily accessed, reputable on-line source for shooters to review the restrictions placed on the AR on both a national and state-by-state basis. If such a thing does, in fact, exist in cyberspace, my research could not uncover that holy grail of information.

I was able to Google a variety of sites that offered bits and pieces of information regarding the legality of the AR, but this subject is, due to the ever-shifting political winds, a moving target. Laws and regulations change. A new law is passed, and then it is amended or it may be found unconstitutional. Sometimes, for whatever reason, some laws exist but aren't enforced. What to do, what to do.

Somewhat dejected by my inability to obtain worthwhile information, I put the question to two pro-gun groups that should know the answer. I asked the National Rifle Association (NRA) and the National Shooting Sports Federation (NSSF). The NSSF is the organization responsible for the effort of trying to change the name of the AR to MSR, an initialism that was to stand for "Modern Sporting Rifle." I can only assume the NSSF's thought was that, if the AR wasn't called an AR—which can be and has often been misconstrued to mean "assault rifle"—then it would no longer pose a menace to society in the minds of the anti-gun movement. Anyway, the NSSF was no help in providing any information about the legal ownership of ARs, other than to suggest contact with the National Rifle Association.

The NRA was indeed helpful, but mostly in a broad sort of way. No doubt the organization knows the specific legality issues of the AR on a state-by-state basis, but I didn't get that information from it. To quote the NRA, "Fitting any group of laws into broad categories is always going to introduce some definitional concerns, but this is the lay of the land. With regards to the question of where ARs are legal, no jurisdiction has said that all ARs are per se illegal. At most, they have come up with lists of banned guns and their copies, as well as gun bans that rely on an action type (usually semi-auto with detachable magazine), plus one or more banned features, such as pistol grips, flash suppressors, bayonet lugs, etc."

Clear as mud? In truth, this is about as

firm as you can nail down the answer to the question, due to the ever-changing legislation proposed and enacted that pertain to the AR firearms system.

One of the issues surrounding the legality of the AR is that the attempts to restrict ownership have focused, as the NRA pointed out, on features of guns in general, as opposed to a specific gun. If you are trying to ban a certain product, this is indeed the way to do it. If you simply try to ban a gun that is named "X," the manufacturers will just change the name to "Y" and continue to sell their product.

The NRA continued, " … It's fair to say that the states we [NRA] list as "legal with restrictions" think they're banning ARs as a general matter (with exceptions for grandfathered guns), but manufacturers and collectors often find a way to make certain design tweaks to comply with the definitions and still give consumers the firearms they want. Thus, manufacturers will often have two versions of the same AR: one that has all the usual features people want and one that conforms to the strictest of the feature tests so that it can be sold in most gun ban jurisdictions."

So, is it legal to own an AR? The response from the NRA is that it is not aware of any jurisdiction where some type of AR-15 isn't legal. However, California, Connecticut, the District of Columbia, Maryland, Massachusetts, New York, and New Jersey do have restrictions that regulate the type or features of the AR that can be legally owned.

One feature of the AR that has wide appeal to shooters is the ability of the platform to utilize high-capacity magazines. AR magazines are available that will hold from five to 100 rounds of ammunition, and eight states have enacted laws regulating the maximum capacity of magazines, regardless the firearm into which they are inserted. Here's that list:

- California: 10 rounds
- Colorado: 15 rounds
- Connecticut: 10 rounds
- District of Columbia: 10 rounds
- Hawaii: 10 Rounds (this law applies only to handguns.)
- Massachusetts: 10 rounds
- New Jersey: 15 rounds
- New York: 10 rounds, but with a seven-round load limit under most circumstances

Now, any of this could change next year or 10 years from now. In fact, as this book is being written, proposed legislation exists in some states and at the national level that would add to this list. Again, the legal ownership of an AR, AR accessories, and all firearms remains a moving target.

What about hunting? Some old-timers and even some old-time gun writers have expressed their disdain for hunting with the AR. No, an AR does not look like the rifle your father or grandfather hunted with; for some, that's enough not to like the AR. Looks have really nothing to do with anything, when it comes to a hunter whose ultimate goal is to successfully take an animal as humanely as possible. Looks, however, have everything to do with emotions and nostalgia.

The good news is, at the time of this writing, no state has a law that prohibits the use of an AR, either by design or definition, for hunting, with one exception; Pennsylvania prohibits hunting with any kind of semi-automatic rifle, ARs included. Too, other states and locales disallow rifles for hunting altogether and, in still others, like Indiana, where a rifle is allowed, there are significant restrictions on the type of cartridge a rifle may fire.

This brings us to the .223 Remington/5.56 NATO cartridge, which is, undeniably, the most common cartridge for which ARs are chambered. The general line

Silence is Golden

As much as the pro-gun crowd is ready to stand up and fight about magazine capacity bans, semi-automatic bans, the ban of lead bullets, and a variety of other things the anti-gun movement would like to make illegal, one thing they need to get behind is suppressor ownership and its legality for hunting. Hearing damage is common among shooters, and very few hunters wear hearing protection when hunting, for obvious reasons. It is indeed a health issue. Suppressor use could eliminate all of this. In fact, in many countries that have much stricter gun laws than the United States, suppressor ownership is *encouraged*, specifically to reduce hearing loss and noise pollution.

you'll hear is that most states will not allow hunters to pursue big-game animals with a .22-caliber centerfire cartridge, and that would include the .223 Remington. This has been repeated so many times that it is almost considered gospel. It was even the opinion of the NRA. But, after talking with many hunters from many states who do use the .223 Remington for deer and other big game, I began to wonder how accurate this statement really was, so I spent several days examining the hunting regulations for all 50 states. I must admit that, in some cases, this was like reading Greek, but, in the end, I found that only 15 out of 50 states prohibit the use of the .223 Remington for deer/big-game hunting. Out of those 15 states, five do not allow the use of rifles of any kind for big-game hunting. In other words, those five states are shotgun-only states. Anyway, consider this myth busted: 35 of the 50 states, a full 70 percent, allow the use of the .223 Remington cartridge for big-game hunting.

On another, quieter note, suppressors are rapidly becoming a very popular AR accessory. Suppressors are easy to attach to most any AR, since most have a threaded muzzle. (Know that ARs with the absence of a threaded muzzle are, to some extent, a response to circumventing anti-AR legislation in some states.) Today, California,

Delaware, the District of Columbia, Hawaii, Illinois, Iowa, Massachusetts, Minnesota, New Jersey, New York, Rhode Island, and Vermont prohibit suppressor ownership. For those states that do allow you to own a suppressor, they are not as difficult to obtain as some may imagine. You have to apply with the BATFE, and that application requires an affidavit from your local law enforcement official, fingerprints, and a $200 tax. After submission, you wait about six months and you'll receive your permit. (Additional restrictions may apply in some locations.)

Aside from their growing popularity, you can even hunt with a suppressor in many states to include Alaska, Arizona, Arkansas, Colorado, Idaho, Kansas, Kentucky, Maryland, Mississippi, Missouri, Nebraska, Nevada, New Mexico, North Dakota, Oklahoma, Oregon, Pennsylvania, South Carolina, South Dakota, Tennessee, Texas, Utah, Virginia, Washington, West Virginia, Wisconsin, and Wyoming. Additionally, Louisiana and Montana allow the use of suppressors for the taking of certain varmints.

When it comes to firearms laws, there is no single or easy answer. Ownership and the ability to purchase and transfer an AR or any firearm will depend on local and federal laws—not the laws that were in effect when this book was written, but the laws that will be in effect at the time of the transfer. The good news is that any reputable gun shop should be abreast of these laws and can advise you accordingly.

One thing to keep in mind is that the lower receiver is the serialized part. That is the part of the AR, per ATF regulations, that's controlled by federal firearms transfer laws. In most states, you can order a complete AR upper receiver by mail and have it shipped directly to your home and not have to be subjected to a background check or any other regulation, as long as that upper receiver meets the legal requirements for ownership in your jurisdiction. All this having been said, I will say again, laws change, so contact your local authorities and check with local dealers before making a purchase of an upper, lower, or anything in between. With that, I'll leave you with some additional advice, courtesy Bushmaster firearms, something that should be headed by any AR owner or prospective owner:

TO ALL BUSHMASTER CUSTOMERS REGARDING VARYING FIREARMS REGULATIONS IN THE U.S.A.

CAUTION! With the "sunset" of the 1994 Assault Weapons Ban on September 13, 2004, Bushmaster can again offer features on the AR-15-type rifle that had been deemed illegal for those 10 years—such as flash suppressors, bayonet lugs, collapsing telescopic stocks, and high capacity magazines. Though that Federal legislation has expired, certain states have retained their own versions of "Assault Weapons Ban" statutes, and prospective Bushmaster buyers should check their own state, county, and city laws to determine the local legality of rifles with these features and accessories.

A STATEMENT FROM BUSHMASTER REGARDING MACHINE GUN PARTS

The position of the Bureau of Alcohol, Tobacco, Firearms and Explosives (BATFE) is that if your AR-15-type rifle contains even one M16 component, it is a machine gun. If you own an AR-15 from any manufacturer, check to make sure there are no M16 components in its assemblies. If there are, remove them immediately. Machine them to AR configuration or replace them and destroy the M16 components. If you have any questions about your parts, give us a call and we'll be glad to supply you with the legally acceptable parts. (800-998-7928; www.bushmaster.com)

CHAPTER 19

COMPANY PROFILES

To sum up a wide collection of companies that manufacturer AR-style rifles, I turned to fellow gun writer Jorge Amselle. While this list is not complete, there is simply no way to list every manufacture or builder of AR-style rifles. The truth is, the gun, being the modular firearm that it is, can be assembled and sold by just about anyone. In fact, at many gun shows, that's exactly what you will find, vendors who have put an AR together using parts from various manufactures. Nonetheless, most shooters want something new, so Jorge and I discussed which companies to include and which ones to leave out. In the end, we settled on 21 companies. If you cannot find an AR you like from one of these manufactures, maybe the AR is not for you.

ADCOR DEFENSE

(www.adcordefense.com)

Adcor Defense, based in Baltimore, Maryland, is a subsidiary of Adcor Industries, Inc., a defense contractor and supplier with more than two decades of experience manufacturing components for the Trident missile and F16 radar systems. Adcor Defense was established to build a new battle rifle for the military and developed the BEAR (Brown Enhanced Automatic Rifle). Today, and though the military has suspended its new rifle development program, Adcor Defense is making a semi-automatic version of the BEAR available for commercial sale.

The BEAR is a fairly significant departure from the traditional AR, although, in appearance and operation, it is nearly identical. This rifle uses a distinct, long-stroke gas piston system of operation, wherein the piston and the bolt carrier are joined together. This ensures the highest level of reliability and completely eliminates any bolt tilt. This system also allows for a fully ambidextrous, non-reciprocating, forward charging handle located above the custom quad-rail handguards. The barrel is available in lengths from 10.5 inches to 18 inches, and the specially designed gas system and handguards allow the barrel to remain free-floated for improved accuracy. The bolt itself is also specially designed to wipe dust and debris away from the ejection port.

Adcor also produces traditional gas impingement rifles with or without the forward charging handle. Caliber selection is currently limited to 5.56mm NATO/.223 Remington. However, 7.62mm NATO and 6.8 SPC variants are in development. Retail prices range from $1,783 to $2,468.

ALEXANDER ARMS
(www.alexanderarms.com)

Alexander Arms was founded, in 2001, in Radford, Virginia, by Bill Alexander, a British expatriate and a former armorer in the UK who has designed various small arms weapon systems, cartridges, and vehicle armor. Alexander Arms is best known for its exotic cartridges. Bill Alexander's interest in cartridge design led him to produce the .50 Beowulf and the 6.5 Grendel, as well as ARs capable of chambering these new cartridges. Most recently, Alexander Arms introduced an AR chambered for the rimfire .17 HMR.

The .50 Beowulf uses a rebated rim to accommodate the AR bolt face and fires a heavy bullet at an intermediate velocity, providing excellent knockdown power against even the largest North American game animals. It is also used by law enforcement for its effectiveness against vehicles, windshield glass, and armor. The 6.5 Grendel, by contrast, is a powerful long-range cartridge similar to the .308, but with half the recoil and in a smaller package.

The company sells a wide variety of complete rifles and carbines, as well as upper receivers and parts and accessories. The uppers and complete guns are available in .50 Beowulf, 6.5 Grendel, .17 HMR, 5.56 NATO/.223 Remington, and .300 AAC Blackout. Prices range from $1,250 to $1,800.

ARMALITE

(www.armalite.com)

Contrary to popular belief, AR does not stand for "assault rifle," it stands for ArmaLite Rifle, the company that first offered the AR. Originally incorporated in 1954, ArmaLite was part of Fairchild Engine and Airplane Corporation and so used the engineering knowledge it acquired from high-tech airplane construction to build the first rifle made from aluminum and composite reinforced fiberglass: the AR-10 chambered in 7.62 mm NATO. This was not the final AR, but it was the synthesis of what would become firearm designer Eugene Stoner's AR-15, his magnum opus.

ArmaLite sold off the rights to the AR-15 to Colt's, but the patents eventually ran out and now anyone can make an AR (Colt's still owns the name). Over the years, ArmaLite has changed hands and locations. Today it is based in Geneseo, Illinois. It was the first to develop a true 7.62mm NATO-chambered AR, a scaled up AR-15 renamed the AR-10B (to avoid confusion with the original AR-10). The full line of AR-10B and AR-10A rifles can be had in a variety of configurations with standard or Magpul furniture and include a military sniper version. These carbines and rifles are available in 7.62 mm NATO, .338 Federal, .243 Winchester, and .260 Remington. The company also makes a standard AR called the M-15, as well as parts and accessories and .22 LR conversion kits. The M-15s are available in several configurations as rifles and carbines and are chambered in 6.8 SPC, 7.62x39mm, and 5.56mm/.223 Remington. Prices range from $989 to $3,100.

BARRETT FIREARMS MANUFACTURING

(www.barrett.net)

In 1982, when Ronnie Barrett started his company in Murfreesboro, Tennessee, it was with one thing in mind: to build a semi-automatic rifle capable of handling the massive .50 BMG round. It was this large, 10-round rifle, the M-82, for which Barrett is best known. Its adoption by the U.S. Military for long-range sniping, and its appearances in feature films, didn't hurt its reputation, either. Since then, Barrett has developed other rifles chambered for this heavy machine-gun round.

It was only in 2007 that Barrett entered the AR market with its version of the classic AR, the REC 7 (Reliability-Enhanced Carbine). This is the only AR-type rifle the company manufactures, and it is built with the same durability and attention to detail as Barrett's .50-caliber rifles. The REC 7 is a carbine-length AR with an easy front access, adjustable gas piston system. The bolt carrier and carrier key are all one piece, to prevent bolt tilt. This rifle is available complete or just as an upper receiver ready for installation in your own lower. Caliber selection is limited to 5.56mm NATO/.223 Remington or 6.8 SPC. This is a premium rifle, as is to be expected from Barrett, and the MSRP is $2,520.

BLACK RAIN ORDNANCE
(www.blackrainordnance.com)

Founded in 2009, in Neosho, Missouri, Black Rain Ordnance, Inc., manufactures high-end ARs using billet upper and lower receivers. The company is best known for the use of innovative muzzle devices and custom-shaped barrels, as well as its distinct biohazard logo and a wide array of finish options and camo patterns. Black Rain Ordnance also uses match-grade stainless steel barrels to achieve sub-MOA performance, and its builds include significant attention to detail style. Billet receivers are CNC-machined out of a solid block of aluminum. This allows for a more uniform receiver that better permits custom features, as opposed to the standard forged receiver wherein the aluminum is pressed into the proper shape.

The company offers complete rifles, stripped upper and lower receiver kits, and parts for both the commercial and law enforcement markets. Chambering options are currently limited to 5.56mm NATO/.223 Remington and 7.62mm NATO/.308 Winchester. Black Rain Ordnance has also expanded to offer its own line of drop-in trigger units for ARs, as well as a full line of pistol and rifle suppressors. Its standard rifles are available with a direct gas impingement system, though gas piston rifles are also offered. Prices for these distinct rifles range from $2,039 to $3,229.

BUSHMASTER
(ww.bushmaster.com)

Founded in 1973, in Windham, Maine, by Richard Dyke, Bushmaster Firearms quickly rose to fame as one of the top AR rifle makers in the world. Indeed, it seems the company's reputation is second only to Colt's. Both company names are inexorably tied to the AR, with the exception that Bushmaster pretty much makes only ARs. Today, the company is headquartered in Madison, North Carolina, while manufacturing is based in Ilion, New York. It shares its ownership with Remington and DPMS, among other firearms companies, under the Freedom Group banner.

Bushmaster ARs have become extremely popular among law enforcement agencies and have a reputation for durability and reliability. While government sales continue as a priority, it also has a very active civilian market. Its designs include AR pistols, rifles, and carbines, as well as carbon fiber models. Bushmaster also sells a full line of parts and accessories for home rifle builders, including complete lower and upper receiver assemblies.

Bushmaster's most common offering is its XM-15 carbine, a standard Mil-Spec rifle built with quality and value in mind. Recognizing that many buyers customize their rifles, Bushmaster also offers an MOE series of carbines with the most popular Magpul furniture installed. Various Cerakote models are available, and its carbon fiber rifles are lightweight and economical. A line of long-range competition and precision rifles is in the lineup, as are big-bore hunting rifles. Popular caliber options include 5.56 NATO/.223 Remington, .22 LR, .308 Winchester/7.62 NATO, 6.8mm Rem SPC, 7.62x39mm, and .300 AAC Blackout. Prices range from $949 to $1,508.

DEL-TON

(www.del-ton.com)

Tony and Kassandra Autry started Del-Ton in their garage, in Elizabethtown, North Carolina, as an AR parts and accessories business that has since expanded to include a full line of complete rifles. Focusing on assembling high-quality parts and materials, Del-Ton offers excellent customer service, outstanding carbines and rifles, and great value. Del-Ton's comprehensive website allows customers to select the specific rifle that fits their needs, and it also includes a huge quantity of parts and accessories. There are complete build kits available for those who want the pleasure of building their own rifle and already have a stripped lower receiver.

With excellent access to the best suppliers and parts and great attention to detail in its rifle builds, Del-Ton also provides the option of customer selected upgrades and parts for a truly custom rifle feel. All its rifles, from the lightweight DT Sport to the DTI Evolution, share many Mil-Spec features and parts. The company offers 20 different models of carbines and full-sized rifles with standard or Magpul furniture. Chambered in 5.56mm only, prices range from $699 to $1,300.

DOUBLESTAR CORP.

(www.star15.com)

Based in Winchester, Kentucky, DoubleStar started as J&T Distributing, that original company named after Jesse and Teresa Starnes, who started the business to sell AR parts and accessories. After more than two decades, the pair decided to start producing their own line of complete AR rifles based on their experience in dealing with high-quality parts. They have also expanded by adding Ace Limited, which makes distinctive and very popular AR stocks, and the DoubleStar Training Academy to their list of companies.

DoubleStar manufactures an extensive list of AR rifles, carbines, and pistols, as well as its own 1911 pistol. Short-barreled rifles for law enforcement and civilian use (with the proper NFA paperwork) are available in 7½-inch, 10½-inch, 11½-inch, and 14½-inch barrel lengths. Carbine ARs include a variety of color furniture options, a patrolman's carbine, and even a zombie model complete with bayonet. A super-lightweight model is also available.

For 3-Gun completion, DoubleStar offers a specialized 18-inch barreled rifle with top features. Full-sized rifles with 20- and 24-inch barrels are offered in camo patterns for hunting, and there are several specialized precision guns. Caliber choices include 5.56mm NATO/.223 Remington, .300 AAC Blackout, 6.5 Grendel, 6.8 SPC, and 9mm. Prices can range between $979 and $1,799 at the top end.

DPMS

(www.dpmsinc.com)

DPMS stands for Defense Procurement Manufacturing Services, the company founded by Randy Luth, in St. Cloud, Minnesota, in 1985. The company originally manufactured parts for military contracts for the M-16 and other weapon systems. It expanded into the civilian market with parts for the AR-15 rifle, eventually growing to include making its own lower receivers and barrels and then complete rifles and carbines for military, law enforcement, competitive shooters, hunters, and the commercial market, and it continues to do so today. In addition to selling complete rifles, the company continues to offer a full line of parts and parts kits, upper and lower receivers, and barrel combinations for the AR enthusiast.

As one of the largest manufacturers of AR-style rifles in the U.S., DPMS is a leader in innovation and produces a wide variety of ARs. Its tactical rifles go from NFA-restricted short-barreled and full-auto weapons to Mil-Spec guns for military and police teams. Specialized ARs also include a series of Tactical Precision rifles for use by dedicated marksmen and snipers. On the civilian side, semi-automatic tactical rifles in a variety of configurations are available, as well as competition rifles, precision rifles, and a full line of hunting and varmint guns. Caliber choices run the gamut and include .223 Remington/5.56 NATO, .300 AAC Blackout, .308 Winchester/7.62 NATO, .204 Ruger, .243 Winchester, .260 Remington, .338 Federal, 6.5 Creedmoor, and 6.8 SPC. DPMS is well known for providing its shooters solid value, with prices ranging from $719 to $2,589.

JP ENTERPRISES, INC.

(www.jprifles.com)

A competitive shooter with nearly four decades of experience, John Paul started JP Enterprises, in White Bear Lake, Minnesota, to sell complete custom rifles and parts. JP is likely best known for developing a side-charging AR-style rifle in .308 Winchester and, later, in .223 Remington. The left-side charging handle is located on the upper receiver and features a self-folding handle above the magazine well. This allows the shooter to manipulate the action, while maintaining a proper hold and cheek weld and never taking the gun off target.

Many of the rifles and carbines produced by JP Enterprises are high-end competition guns with a reputation for extreme accuracy, but other models are designed for tactical, personal protection, hunting, and long-range precision purposes. The company has also expanded into traditional, top-charging AR manufacturing and even has a hybrid rifle that combines both the top-charging T-handle and its proprietary side-charging system for ultimate versatility. Side-charging upper receivers are also available to install on your own lower. Other models include a blowback-operated 9mm carbine and a .22 LR rifle for more economical shooting. Caliber options include .223 Remington, .204 Ruger, 6.5 Grendel, .308 Winchester, .260 Remington, 6.5 Creedmoor, and .338 Federal. As premium and custom rifles, prices range from $2,200 to $4,000.

KNIGHTS ARMAMENT

(www.knightsarmco.com)

Knight's Armament Company was founded by C. Reed Knight, in Titusville, Florida, in 1982. It specializes in the production of the highest quality AR rifles for select military units. The company is best known for its innovative weapon systems and accessory designs, including a handguard rail interface system that simplifies the process of adding accessories and mission critical equipment to the rifle.

Eugene Stoner, inventor of the AR, joined the company in 1990, and further improved and refined his original design. Stoner then led the development of a new 7.62mm NATO AR named the SR-25, a model later adopted as a standard sniper rifle by the U.S. Navy SEALs. Stoner next turned his attention to improving the AR-15 and, so, developed the SR-15 that many consider to be the finest of all AR variants, one including an improved bolt design that delivers increased reliability and durability over standard ARs. Stoner stayed at Knights Armament working on rifle development until his death, in 1997.

Today, the company continues to produce accessories, parts, complete rifles, and upper receivers for the military and civilian market. Its rifle categories include the original SR-25 in 7.62mm NATO/.308 Winchester, as well as the SR-15 chambered in 5.56mm NATO/.223 Remington. The only other option is the SR-30, which is chambered for the increasingly popular .300 AAC Blackout. Prices for base rifles can range between $2,200 and $2,750.

LEWIS MACHINE & TOOL COMPANY

(www.lewismachine.net)

In 1980, Karl Lewis started Lewis Machine & Tool Company, headquartered in Milan, Illinois. The company manufactures complete weapons systems and parts for the military and government agencies, including the M-16 and M203. It is best known, however, for its development of the monolithic rail platform, a one-piece upper receiver that combines the usually separate handguard and upper receiver into a single unit for added strength and durability and which includes a quick-change barrel system and a free-floating barrel.

It was this system that LMT incorporated into its LM 308M WS rifle chambered in 7.62mm NATO/.308 Winchester. The inherent durability and versatility of the rifle, as well as its outstanding accuracy, led to its adoption as a standard-issue designated marksman rifle by the British army. The version of this rifle available in the U.S. varies slightly from the UK model.

Customers can purchase traditional gas impingement rifles and carbines or piston operated firearms with or without the monolithic rail platform and quick-change barrel system. Different barrel lengths are available in blackened stainless or chrome-moly, and there is a complete sharpshooters weapon system offered. Caliber choices include 7.62mm NATO/.308 Winchester, 5.56mm NATO/.223 Remington, 6.8 SPC, and .300 Whisper, and prices can range from $1,371 for a base rifle to $5,197 for a complete rifle system.

MOSSBERG
(www.mossberg.com)

O.F. Mossberg & Sons is another company that surprised many, when it entered the AR market. It was founded, in 1919, in North Haven, Connecticut, by Oscar Frederick Mossberg, a native of Sweden, and his sons. The company made a name for itself producing sporting rifles and shotgun, as well other outdoor equipment and sporting goods. It remains a family owned and run business to this day—indeed, it is the longest continually operated and family run firearms company in the U.S.

Mossberg is probably best known for manufacturing the fastest selling shotgun in history, the Mossberg 500, with more than 10 million produced since its introduction, in 1961. With a variety of models available, there is also a version adopted for official duty use by the U.S. military. Today, Mossberg continues to make rifles and shotguns with a well-earned reputation for quality and value.

Only very recently has Mossberg started producing AR-type rifles. Called the MMR (Mossberg Modern Rifle), two versions are currently available. The first is the MMR Hunter, which comes optics ready (no sights) and with a smooth aluminum handguard that leaves the 20-inch rifle barrel free-floating for improved accuracy. This rifle is available in black or two different Mossy Oak camouflage patterns. The MMR Tactical Carbine is available only in black and includes a collapsible stock and a free-floated barrel with a quad-rail handguard. The 16-inch barrel also has a flash hider. Both rifles include the distinct Stark SE-1 pistol grip with an internal battery compartment and integral extended trigger guard. Caliber choice is limited to 5.56mm NATO/.223 Remington and the standard MSRP is $978.

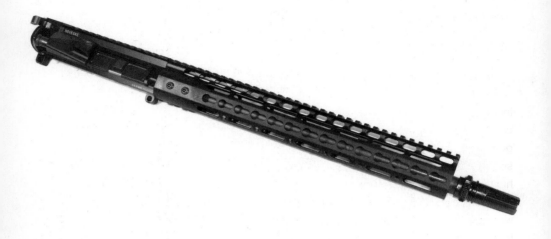

NOVESKE RIFLEWORKS, LLC

(www.noveskerifleworks.com)

After serving in the military, John Noveske went to work as a machinist for a rifle builder. Eventually, he started his own company in his parents' garage, in Grants Pass, Oregon. Noveske developed the switch-block gas regulating system for use with suppressed rifles, to improve their functioning and reliability. Noveske ARs have an overall well-earned reputation for extreme quality, which is something John Noveske always emphasized in the build of each rifle. Sadly, Noveske passed away in 2013, the victim of a motor vehicle accident. He was barely in his mid-30s. His company, thankfully, lives on, and the people whom he trained and hired are just as committed to quality as he had been.

Ordering a rifle from Noveske is truly a custom experience. The buyer must select the caliber first, then the barrel type in either stainless steel or the more traditional chrome lined and cold hammer forged. The stainless barrels can be had in lengths ranging between 7½ inches and 18 inches and have a proprietary chambering, button rifling, and improved accuracy. The chrome-lined cold hammer forged barrels come only in 10½- and 16-inch lengths, but feature twice the standard chrome lining of other AR barrels for extreme durability.

Several completed rifles are available for each category, and calibers include 5.56mm NATO/.223 Remington, .300 AAC Blackout, and 6.8 SPC. Barrels, parts, and accessories, as well as complete upper assemblies, are also available. Prices for completed rifles range from $1,835 to $2,790.

REMINGTON

(www.remington.com)

Eliphalet Remington founded the Remington Arms Company, LLC, in Ilion, New York, in 1816. It is the oldest American firearms company still in operation, and it makes both guns and ammunition. While Big Green, as it is sometimes called, is best known for producing hunting shotguns and bolt-action rifles, it is now a full participant in the AR market. This was largely a result of its joint ownership with longtime AR makers Bushmaster and DPMS.

The Remington autoloading Model R-15 was primarily intended to capture the hunting market for ARs. Several versions of the R-15 are offered in a variety of camo patterns and with collapsible or fixed stocks, 18- and 22-inch barrels, and with upgraded furniture from Magpul. Two-stage target triggers are standard. The R-15 is available in .223 Remington, .30 Remington AR, .450 Bushmaster, and .204 Ruger. MSRP range from $1,276 to $1,327.

For big-bore hunting, Remington also offers the R-25 chambered in a choice of .243 Winchester, 7mm-08 Remington, and .308 Winchester. It comes with a free floated 20-inch barrel and, as it is with all of Remington's AR offering, no sights are included, as the rifles are intended to be used with optics. MSRP on the R-25 is $1,631.

ROCK RIVER ARMS

(www.rockriverarms.com)

As is often the case, experience and knowledge gained in one place lead the entrepreneur to go it alone. Rock River Arms is just such an example. Founded in 1996, in Colona, Illinois, by brothers Mark and Chuck Larson after the two had endured stints with other firearms manufacturers, the company began making 1911 pistols. Production of AR-type rifles and carbines soon followed, and the brothers quickly gained a reputation for quality, innovation, and value. Indeed, Rock River Arms is one of very few AR manufacturers making left-handed models, where the ejection and controls on the upper receiver are reversed from their standard configuration. Most notably, in 2003, the Rock River Arms LAR-15 rifle was selected, after an extensive trial, as the issue carbine for the Drug Enforcement Administration (DEA).

Today, the company makes a full line of complete AR pistols, rifles, and carbines and is reentering the 1911 market with a polymer-framed pistol. It also sells an extensive line of parts and accessories, including complete upper and lower receivers. In addition to ARs in right- and left-handed versions, customers can select direct gas impingement operation or gas piston operation.

Customers have a wide choice of calibers, including 5.56mm NATO/.223 Remington, 7.62mm NATO/.308 Winchester, 6.8 SPC, .458 SOCOM, and carbines in 9mm and .40 S&W. Most recently, Rock River Arms has introduced an AR chambered for the Russian 7.62x39mm cartridge and which is modified to accept most standard AK magazines. Prices range from $1,010 to $1,740.

SMITH & WESSON

(www.smith-wesson.com)

Smith & Wesson is certainly a known entity with shooters worldwide. It was founded to make an innovative lever-action pistol, in 1852, in Springfield, Massachusetts, by Horace Smith and Daniel B. Wesson. The pair's real success, however, came with revolvers and, later, pistols. In 2006, the company took a decidedly bold step by introducing its own line of AR-style rifles, the M&P15 series. The M&P name, which stands for Military and Police, has its own provenance in Smith & Wesson lore, as this was also the name of one of its most popular revolvers.

The M&P15 rifles and carbines are available in a variety of configurations, including many state-compliant models to account for the various feature restrictions some states impose. In addition to standard carbines, which have gained popularity among law enforcement, Smith & Wesson also offers camouflage versions for hunting use, along with others having upgraded Magpul furniture. A varmint rifle is also available. Many of the models feature distinct 1:8 twist barrels with 5R rifling. Centerfire caliber choices are limited to 5.56 NATO/.223 Remington and .300 Whisper/.300 AAC Blackout, but, in 2009, the company introduced the M&P 15-22 chambered in .22LR. Smith & Wesson also sells upper receivers and a full line of accessories. Prices start at $499 for the M&P15-22 and at $839 for the standard M&P15 and can rise to $1,949 for special signature models.

SPIKES TACTICAL
(www.spikestactical.com)

Founded in 2001, in Apopka, Florida, Spike's Tactical has a reputation for building very high-quality ARs, as well as innovative parts and accessories. This includes its own line of polymer 30-round magazines, as well as the extensive use of nickel-boron coating on bolt carrier groups and other parts. NiB-X nickel-boron is a compound harder than chrome (Rc70 hardness), yet has less friction (similar to Teflon), while also providing extreme corrosion resistance and natural lubricity.

Spike's Tactical also manufactures an ST-T1 buffer, which is CNC-machined from solid billet of aluminum bar stock and filled with tungsten powder. This eliminates the rattle of traditional metal disks used as buffer weights and provides for smooth cycling. The company also manufactures top-end quad-rail handguards in different lengths and weights. All the rifles currently offered are limited to 16-inch carbines and short-barreled rifles, including one with an integral suppressor. In the past, it did offer a wider variety of options with longer barrels and more custom work, and things are now available on special order.

The current offering focuses on the needs of personal-defense, law enforcement, and competition, and caliber choices are limited to 5.56mm NATO/.223 Remington and .300 AAC Blackout. Given the guns' reputations for quality and Mil-Spec features, pricing is very competitive, ranging from $950 to $2,750.

STAG ARMS

(www.stagarms.com)

Mark Malkowski founded Stag Arms, in New Britain, Connecticut, in 2003, but the company has stated that it will move to a more gun-friendly state in the near future. The company is best known for its development of left-handed ARs. In these models, the upper receiver has been mirrored so that the forward assist and ejection port are on the left side. The dust cover rotates upward, and the bolts and bolt carrier have also been adjusted for left hand ejection. When combined with an ambidextrous safety, bolt, magazine release, and charging handle, the rifle can become fully left-hand compatible.

Stag Arms sells complete rifles and carbines in right-hand and left-hand versions, as well as complete right- and left-hand upper receivers and standard lower receivers and parts and accessories. The company states it manufactures 80 percent of its parts in-house and provides an infinite shot guarantee on its barrels. Among the available options are carbines and rifles, as well as tactical and 3-Gun competition models. A varmint hunting model is also available, as are piston-operated versions. Caliber choices are limited to 5.56mm NATO/.223 Remington and 6.8 SPC. Stag Arms ARs are well made and innovative, while still offering good value. Prices range from $940 to $1,500.

STURM, RUGER & COMPANY
(www.ruger.com)

It seems that no firearms company can avoid competing in the exponentially popular AR market these days. Originally founded in 1949, by William B. Ruger and Alexander McCormick Sturm, in Southport, Connecticut, Sturm, Ruger & Company, or just plain Ruger, as it is most commonly known, made a name for itself with Bill Ruger's .22 caliber semi-automatic pistol that copied the looks of a German Luger. The company's next great success was also in the rimfire market, this time with its 10/22 rifle. Like the Mark I pistol, the 10/22 rifle became one of the most successful rimfire guns ever made.

Ruger's first modern tactical rifle was the popular Mini-14, a version of the military M-14 chambered in 5.56mm NATO/.223 Remington. But, when the company decided to enter the AR market, it decided that making the same rifle as everyone else wasn't an option. So it introduced its own take on the AR, the SR-556. This series of rifles and carbines is available only with a two-stage gas piston system, and the guns carry on the company's reputation for extreme durability. Variations include a standard carbine with quad-rail handguards, and a more economical version with a modified handguard. A varmint hunting long-barreled version is also offered. Caliber selection is limited to 5.56mm NATO/.223 Remington, but a separate upper receiver assembly is available in 6.8 SPC. Prices range from $1,375 to $1,995.

WILSON COMBAT

(www.wilsoncombat.com)

Bill Wilson started out in the family business as a jeweler working on precision timepieces. On the side, he got involved in competitive shooting. In 1977, Wilson decided to combine his passion for firearms and his skills as a jeweler and started Wilson Combat, gunsmithing and, eventually, manufacturing top-of-the-line custom 1911 pistols, the work done almost completely by hand. Based in Berryville, Arkansas, the company has expanded into the custom tactical shotgun and AR markets with significant success and now also manufacturers high-quality ammunition.

Wilson Combat ARs have the same level of extreme build quality and attention to detail as do the company's famed pistols, but this level of quality comes at a premium. Base prices range from $2,250 to $2,600 and can increase rapidly with extra options. These rifles are built for hard duty use, reliability, and precision and are tested extensively by Wilson himself on his ranch against a large population of feral hogs.

In addition to signature models such as the Paul Howe Tactical Carbine, Wilson also offers a full line of other carbines and rifles for tactical and suppressed use, as well as short-barreled models. The company also makes a high-end intermediate designated marksman rifle and a Super Sniper heavy barrel gun suitable for hunting or tactical applications. Available calibers include 5.56 NATO, 6.8 SPC, .300 AAC Blackout, .458 SOCOM, and Wilson's own 7.62x40WT.

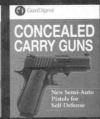